TEA-
VITALIZE

TEA-VITALIZE

Cold Brew
Teas and
Herbal
Infusions to
Refresh and
Rejuvenate

Mimi Kirk

PHOTOGRAPHS BY MIKE MENDELL

THE COUNTRYMAN PRESS
A division of W. W. Norton & Company
Independent Publishers Since 1923

I BELIEVE HEALTH IS IN YOUR REFRIGERATOR,
NOT IN YOUR MEDICINE CABINET.

For information about permission to reproduce selections from this book, write to
Permissions, The Countryman Press, 500 Fifth Avenue, New York, NY 10110

For information about special discounts for bulk purchases, please contact
W. W. Norton Special Sales at specialsales@wwnorton.com or 800-233-4830

Manufacturing by Versa Press
Photographs by Mike Mendell, unless otherwise indicated
Illustrations by Carolyn Kelly
Production manager: Devon Zahn

The Countryman Press
www.countrymanpress.com

A division of W. W. Norton & Company, Inc.
500 Fifth Avenue, New York, NY 10110
www.wwnorton.com

978-1-68268-283-8 (pbk.)

10 9 8 7 6 5 4 3 2 1

CONTENTS

COLD BREW HERBAL INFUSIONS 75

HOT HERBAL INFUSIONS 97

COLD BREW FRUIT INFUSIONS   135

FRUIT HOT WATER INFUSIONS   151

INTRODUCTION

My passion is to lead a healthy, happy life and to provide the best information I can to help others do the same. I am always searching for and researching new and ancient traditions that can recharge health, happiness, and everyday life. Adding more good habits into our lives will also help release any bad habits and, in turn, will allow us to balance body, mind, and spirit.

I've known the benefits of plants and herbs for a long time. I've used them for many decades to keep my family, friends, clients, and myself healthy. I've written books about plant food, spoken internationally, and been on national television praising the importance of plant food. I feel consuming plants slowed down my aging process, rid me of high blood pressure and cholesterol, and has kept me prescription-free and energetic at the age of eighty.

In my book *H₂Oh!* I taught readers how to make some of my favorite fresh filtered water infusions, but I'm not finished trying to keep you hydrated. This book will expand on what you learned in *H₂Oh!* and guide you into some surprisingly positive healing methods.

The recipes in *Tea-Vitalize* are easy and fun to make, and are all superdelicious. Best of all, they have medicinal properties to boost your immunity and help you stay healthy in many ways.

Tea-Vitalize will enlighten you in such a simple way that you will be surprised you didn't know about the benefits of tea before, and if you did know, this book will renew your passion and inspire you to stay on a path of ultimate health and self-love.

To help you understand more of what *Tea-Vitalize* is about, imagine taking a hot shower or soaking in a warm bath on a cold day. It feels soothing, right? If it's a hot day, imagine bathing in a cool lake or swimming under a waterfall. Your body immediately cools down from the heat when surrounded by cool water. If you can imagine your body feeling so good on the outside, I'm going to show you how to experience the same feelings on the inside—and all it takes is the proper kind of hydration. *Tea-Vitalize* offers

simple recipes and formulas that will enable you to drink refreshing, luscious, healthy cold liquids on hot days and soothing warm liquids on cold days. In no time at all, you will be creating your own tasty drinks and feeling like a million bucks.

Health is wealth, and hydration is life-giving. In *Tea-Vitalize*, you will learn the benefits of hydration, how to properly hydrate, and how to make endless mouthwatering drinks to help prevent illness, balance weight, support your immune system, and take your health to a whole new level.

Although a fundamental component to good health is staying hydrated, many people forget to drink water and instead reach for sugary drinks and coffee when they get thirsty or need a boost. By the time you feel thirsty, you are already dehydrated, and sugary drinks only add to the dehydration. Research says we cannot survive very long without water: harm is done in a matter of days, when our body's organs start to shut down.

Most of us have heard we should drink eight 8-ounce glasses of water per day. But the Health and Medicine Division of the National Academy of Medicine says we should be drinking more than that: men should be drinking on average thirteen glasses a day (104 ounces); and women, nine glasses (72 ounces). Activity level, weather, and age could also help determine our optimal water intake. It's not exactly the same for everyone. Some studies say we should be drinking about half our body weight in ounces of filtered water daily. For example, a person who weighs 140 pounds should drink 70 ounces of water (or other hydrating, non-sugary fluids) daily. That's 2 quarts plus ¾ cup. If you take medication or have specific health issues, such as kidney or heart failure, check with your health-care professional, as you may require less water. Always check with your doctor if you are pregnant or breastfeeding, whenever adding new foods or drinks to your diet.

To help encourage you to drink enough liquids daily, here are some ways dehydration can affect us: it makes weight loss more difficult and causes mental confusion, slow memory, fatigue, lack of attention and focus, accumulations of toxins, digestive issues, urinary infections, inflammation, and much more.

Proper hydration removes toxins, lubricates our body, reduces electric and magnetic field (EMF) exposure, and increases electrolytes. It helps with absorption of nutrients, removes waste, regulates blood pressure and body temperature, and slows down biological aging.

Drinking water and staying hydrated is important to our health, but what if I told you that you could infuse your water with something that would improve your health far beyond hydration? And what if I told you this something was tea and herbal infusions?

I know you may be picturing sitting down to a cup of hot tea, as that's what many people visualize when they think of tea, but stay with me here. This is not your grandmother's cup-and-saucer kind of tea (not that there is anything is wrong with that). *Tea-Vitalize* will introduce you to a cool, modern way to consume tea without boiling water.

Tea replaces lost fluid in the body, and contains potent antioxidants as well. Both water and tea are good for us and this book is all about helping you drink more tasty fluids to stay hydrated and healthy.

Claims that tea can improve your health come from ancient religious and spiritual texts all the way to modern medical journals. While we wait for more scientific results, there is no harm in drinking teas and herbal infusions. In fact, drinking at least 32 ounces of tea or herbal infusion daily may be better than drinking the same amount of water because of the added nutrients teas and herbal infusions provide. Herbal infusions contain antioxidants, which are important to maintaining good health. Teas and herbs speak to our body in a completely natural way and they are soothing to our mind as well.

In addition, numerous teas and herbal infusions are said to promote healing. I have spent hundreds of hours researching the claims in this book and they are widely documented. That said, I'm not a doctor and the recipes in this book are not meant to give or replace medical advice from your health-care professional. If you are interested in any of the findings I talk about, speak to your health-care professional before treating any health condition with teas or herbs. And do research these topics for yourself, as you will find information abundantly available.

Here's how I see it: we all know fruits, vegetables, and herbs have health benefits. The true teas (see page 37) along with herbal infusions (from any plants besides the true teas), fall into the same category as fruits and vegetables. True tea and herbal infusions come from the fruits, flowers, leaves, stems, bark, and roots of plants so it makes sense that teas made from these plants share their health benefits. For example, green tea is known to contain antioxidants and flavonoids. Also, some teas and herbs are known to be antimicrobial and anti-inflammatory.

In ancient Greece, Egypt, China, and India, centuries-old traditions make positive claims about the benefits of teas and herbs in the treatment of numerous diseases and illnesses. Even if these benefits are not accepted by the scientific community at the present time, it does not mean we should rule out ancient wisdom, herbalism, Ayurveda, or alternative medicine, which all helps keep our body in balance and harmony via herbal infusions and teas.

Some years ago I helped create a fundraiser with singer-songwriter Sting to support the Kayapo tribe in saving the Amazon rain forest from deforestation and destruction. I met Kayapo chief Raoni Metuktire, who lives deep in the Amazon rain forest in Brazil. He told me—through his interpreter—that his tribe has to keep moving deeper into the forest as the trees are being cut down for cattle grazing and logging. In his forest, he said, "there are thousands of plants that heal many diseases, and now many of these plants are destroyed because of deforestation." He continued, "If only people would explore and use these natural plants, many diseases would be cured or prevented." He then pulled a folded, tattered paper from his pocket. He unfolded what turned out to be a large map and spread it out on the table. He pointed to a spot and said, "When I was a boy, the forest went from here to there"—and he showed me a very wide span of forest—"but now," he said, "the forest only stretches from here to here," and he indicated a much smaller part of the remaining rain forest. It was a shockingly minute area. He then said, "When the trees are gone, people will not be able to breathe."

Chief Raoni's words struck me deeply, as I've been an environmentalist for decades and I know the rain forest is home to much of the world's biodiversity. According to the World Wildlife Fund, rain forests "soak up carbon dioxide . . . that would otherwise be free in the atmosphere and contribute to ongoing changes in climate patterns and air quality," and "We are losing 18.7 million acres of forests annually, equivalent to 27 soccer fields every minute." If we don't respect the power of plants and trees, we will continue to get further away from attaining our own good health as well as our planet's health.

The Social History of Tea

Tea is the most widely consumed beverage in the world after water. For centuries, tea has been a valued medicinal elixir revered for its health benefits. Drinking tea is a holistic approach to treating disease and illness. Tea can soothe the mind and body, it eases nervous tension and stress, and its aroma can lift our spirits. During the summer months in California, sun tea was always brewing on our patio. When we were sick or needed a lift, a hot cup of tea was always around to warm us and make us feel cared for.

Many people think the British discovered tea, as they are big tea drinkers, but it wasn't until around 1664 that tea was introduced to Great Britain. In fact, the birth of tea occurred in China. A legend claims that around 2700 BCE, the emperor Shen

Nung was sitting beneath a tree where his servant was boiling drinking water. A few leaves from the tree above dropped into the boiling water. Shen Nung, a renowned herbalist, decided to try the drink that had accidentally been created. The tree was a *Camellia sinensis* and the resulting drink was what we now call tea. True story or not, tea became popular in China centuries before it was ever heard of in the West. Tea containers were found in tombs dating from the Han dynasty (206 BCE–220 AD). Under the Tang dynasty (618–907 AD), tea became established as the national drink of China. Tea also became a vital part of Japanese culture, introduced to Japan by Japanese Buddhist monks who studied in China.

The Science of Tea

Archaeological evidence indicates that the use of medicinal plants dates back to the Paleolithic age, approximately 60,000 years ago.

I could write a book on the many studies done on tea, as scientists seem to be fascinated with its medicinal possibilities. The scientific community is familiar with the many claims made by ancient cultures that follow centuries-old traditions and praise the medicinal cures from drinking tea.

The health properties of teas may vary depending on where the plants are grown and how the teas are processed, stored, brewed, and consumed. With regard to processing, for instance, green tea is rich in catechins, whereas in black tea the catechins convert into other compounds during fermentation. In another example, brewing time can cause various polyphenols to have different effects on the body. In cold brew teas, the longer steeping time results in more polyphenols being released. However, in hot teas, steeping for longer than suggested doesn't significantly increase these compounds. And when tea is decaffeinated or bottled commercially, it usually contains lower levels of polyphenols. Even where the tea is consumed matters: some Asian studies find certain benefits whereas Western ones do not, and vice versa. This may be in part because our genes and our colonic microflora—the bacteria living in our large intestine—also help determine what effects tea has on our body, pointing to the influence of our overall diet upon the benefits we may expect from drinking tea.

Many of the claims made regarding the healing power of tea are due to the compounds found in tea, including high antioxidant properties and flavonoids. These claims include improved heart health, better digestion, oral heath, lower cholesterol, lower blood pressure, improved memory, weight loss, improved immunity, and decreased tumors, to name a few. What we do know for sure is that tea contains hundreds of biologically active chemicals that can be absorbed and used by the body to varying degrees.

An article, "Tea and Cancer Prevention," which appears on the National Cancer Institute website, states:

> Among their many biological activities, the predominant polyphenols in green tea . . . and the types of catechin and the theaflavins and thearub-igins in black teas have antioxidant activity. These chemicals have sub-stantial free radical scavenging activity and may protect cells from DNA damage caused by reactive oxygen species. Tea polyphenols have also been shown to inhibit tumor cell proliferation and induce apoptosis. . . . In other laboratory studies tea catechins have been shown to inhibit angio-genesis and tumor cell invasiveness. In addition, tea polyphenols may protect against damage caused by ultraviolet (UV) B radiation, and they may modulate immune system function. Furthermore, green teas have been shown to activate detoxification enzymes, such as glutathione S-transferase and quinone reductase, that may help protect against tumor development.

Although many of the potential beneficial effects of tea have been attributed to the strong antioxidant activity of tea polyphenols, the precise mechanism by which tea might help prevent cancer has not been established.

According to Cancer Research UK, although there is no concrete evidence as yet that green tea can help with cancer, some people drink it because they believe it might boost their immune system, which could help them fight their cancer or improve health, energy levels, and well-being, or detoxify their body.

There is some evidence from early studies to suggest the possibility that drinking green tea may reduce the risk of getting cancer, perhaps due to its epigallocatechin-3-gallate (EGCG, a potent antioxidant) content, but at the moment, the evidence is not strong enough to know this for sure.

More recently, along with green tea, black tea is being promoted as possibly being an anticancer agent. Black tea comes from the same plant as green tea, but black tea is made from the fermented leaves of the plant.

Aside from cancer, claims have been made for centuries that teas have helped cure a variety of diseases. Researchers are very interested in the subject and thousands of papers have been written leaning both pro and con. For example, dozens of review papers from the Fifth International Scientific Symposium on Tea and Human Health, held in Washington, DC, in 2017, were published in the *American Journal of Clinical Nutrition*. These papers drew largely on the more than 2,000 studies done on tea in just the past few years.

According to Jeffrey Blumberg, PhD, professor of nutrition science at Tufts University and chairman of the tea symposium, "Of all the potential benefits of tea, those involving cardiovascular disease are 'the most promising.'"

The University of California, Berkeley, states in its Wellness Newsletter that many observational studies have found that people who consume moderate (4 to 5 cups) or high amounts (6 or more cups) of green or black tea per day have a reduced risk of cardiovascular disease and stroke. Furthermore, most research has shown that tea can slightly lower LDL (bad) cholesterol and blood pressure, as well as improve blood vessel functioning, reduce inflammation, inhibit blood clotting, and have other positive cardiovascular effects.

Although there is disparity in testing results, it is agreed that polyphenols and flavonoids in true teas improve endothelial function—the function of the lining inside the blood vessels, cardiac valves, and other body cavities. Also, tea's beneficial effects on factors affecting bone mass may help protect against osteoporosis. According to a study published in *Molecular Aspects of Medicine*, flavonoids from either green or black tea prevent the buildup of plaque inside the arteries. Thus, black tea is associated with reduced risk of cardiovascular disease. Medicine Plus rates black tea as possibly effective for reducing the risk of hardening of the arteries, especially in women. Green tea consumption received high marks for postmenopausal women.

Another study published in *BMJ Open* looked at data from 50 countries and found that high consumption of black tea was strongly associated with a reduced diabetes risk. And a Chinese meta-analysis of clinical trials suggested that green tea helps reduce blood sugar.

An analysis of data from the large National Health and Nutrition Examination Survey linked tea consumption with lower weight and smaller waist size. Drinking more tea can act as a diuretic, and drinking tea instead of grabbing a sugary drink or food when you are not really hungry could account for the loss of weight.

A Japanese study in China tested older people who regularly drank green tea. They were found to have a reduced risk of cognitive impairment compared to non-tea-drinkers.

Tea may also help enhance concentration and learning ability because of its amino acid theanine and thiamine (vitamin B$_1$), which also promotes relaxation. At least two other Japanese studies claim that drinking tea reduced the risk of tooth loss. Research shows tea has antibacterial effects, which may reduce levels of bacteria that cause cavities and contribute to gum disease. It could be the natural fluoride in tea that promotes good teeth and gum health.

Two studies were done on the effects of black tea on Parkinson's disease. One study, published in the *American Journal of Epidemiology*, claims people who drank black tea—but not green tea—had a much lower risk of Parkinson's than did non-tea-drinkers. The second study, published in the *Annual Review of Nutrition*, suggests that the compounds in tea may help protect against Parkinson's and other neuro-degenerative diseases.

In all the studies I've read, many positive claims have been made regarding tea. It would be a mistake to ignore thousands of years of accumulated traditional wisdom indicating that tea, a member of the plant kingdom, can heal and prevent many diseases and illnesses. It is agreed that all teas contain phytochemicals, key ingredients in fruits and vegetables, which we already know are part of a healthy diet. According to the Tea Association of the USA, millions of tea drinkers say they are aware of the health benefits of drinking tea.

I believe wholeheartedly in the power of tea and herbal infusions, but there are no magic bullets. If you eat a bad diet and drink tea, it's still a bad diet.

INFUSIONS 101

Infused Waters

I consider tea a water infusion. Water is first infused with loose tea or tea bags and then fruit or herbs can be added for a further infusion. My favorite way to enjoy tea is Cold Brew Refrigerator Tea (page 168). I thought I invented this technique and told my family of my discovery. After months of consuming my cold brew tea, I was surprised to find out it was already a "thing," but that didn't stop me from continuing to create my own special brews.

You can find cold iced teas in the cooler at your supermarket or coffee shop, but they are not the same as homemade cold brew tea—remember, commercial teas are processed and some contain sugar and artificial flavoring. Nothing tastes as good as homemade. Plus, it takes seconds to make and costs pennies.

Infused water has been around for decades, but recently it has become a trend, one I feel will be around for many years to come. Infused water is what occurs when fruits, vegetables, or herbs are added to filtered water or a tea infusion. To make a cold brew tea infusion, loose tea or tea bags are added to filtered room temperature water and brewed in the refrigerator for six hours or overnight. They are slow infusions that extract all the benefits of the leaves without harming the antioxidants. Slow infusions make a smooth tea with a less acidic taste. Fruit may be added when the bagged or loose tea is removed. When drinking cold brew, remember to not expect a sugary drink taste; it's more like drinking flavored water.

I honestly can't wait to teach you how to make my favorite cold brew refrigerator teas, which are delicious, healthy, and easy to make. Even if you've never cared for tea, cold brew could change your mind. Anyone can make this drink, even a person who can't boil water. At a recent retreat in Mallorca, Spain, where I was teaching classes, there were students from all around the world. Tea was a drink some participants never cared for, but once they tried cold brew, they all carried their jar of tea around from morning to night, filling it up from the large spigot jars of assorted teas. By the end of the week, students said they were "hooked." I continue to get e-mails and photos from many of the students who continue to drink cold brew tea daily.

Hot water tea infusions are made with water that is lightly boiled and infused with herbs, tea bags or loose tea, and fruit. They are medicinal and soothing on a cold day.

I think you will find making tea water so simple that it just might become your daily drink of choice. Try drinking my cold brew teas daily for one week and you will start to crave them. They are a perfect addiction for any health-minded person. In the evening, fill a wineglass with cold brew tea, add some infused ice cubes (see page 171) and a bit of citrus or other fruit, and sip your way to health.

WHAT IS THE BEST WATER TO USE FOR INFUSIONS?

The water you consume is very important. Filtered water is best. Filtered water can come from a home unit under the sink, a countertop unit, or one built into your refrigerator. Each is much better than water purchased in plastic bottles. Plastic bottles can leech chemicals and plastic into the water, and some bottled water is just glorified tap water. Bisphenol A (BPA) bottles can release bisphenol S (BPS), which can contaminate the liquid, according to Cheryl Watson, PhD, a biochemist at the University of Texas Medical Branch at Galveston who's done extensive research on human exposure to BPA and BPS. Plastic chemicals can raise your risk of heart disease; refilling plastic bottles can increase your risk of harmful bacteria and expose you to carcinogens; and last but not least, they are terrible for the environment.

Different filters remove different impurities from the water. Do your research to find out which is best for your household needs in the area where you live. I currently use a stainless steel Berkey water system, and I love it. The Berkey system filters out contaminates from municipal tap water, but can also turn any fresh water source into clean drinking water by removing harmful heavy metals, pharmaceuticals, pesticides, and more. It's convenient as sits on the kitchen countertop and looks beautiful. Berkey has sports bottles as well, which are good for travel and daily use outside the home. The Berkey was recently used after a hurricane in Puerto Rico to turn muddy waters into drinking water. For more information, check out YouTube videos showing muddy water run through a Berkey, coming out clean and clear. Always do your homework when purchasing any products to see whether they are right for you. For more information about the Berkey system, visit www.berkeywater.com.

If you've ever wondered whether boiling water for tea was harmful to the structure of water or what the proper boiling point for the best cup of tea might be, then you will enjoy what I found in a book from 760 AD called *The Classic of Tea*, by Lu Yu, a Chinese writer and tea master. This small book was the first treatise on tea, written during the Tang dynasty (618–907 AD). The original work was lost and the earliest available editions date from the Ming dynasty (1368–1644 AD).

Besides water temperature, the cultivation, soil, and the time of year that tea leaves are grown and harvested were all important to Lu Yu for the proper way of making and consuming tea. He said preparing tea is an important ritual and a ceremony. He detailed exactly how to heat water for tea: "When boiling water, if the bubbles are the size of small fish eyes, with a bit of sound, this is the first boil. When the water around the side of the pot is pearl size bubbles and sounds like an energetic spring, this is the second boil. When the water is raging like stormy turbulent waves, this is the third boil. At the third boil, the water is considered old, and should not be used."

Before reading his book, I always made sure my water boiled fully, but since Lu Yu was a revered tea master, I now use water from the first little bubbles or the second pearl-size bubbles to make hot tea. Prolonged boiling or old water is not recommended. Whether making cold brew or hot tea, there is beauty and calmness in the ritual of making tea. For me, it is taking a few moments of time for self-care.

Tests have been conducted on stovetop boiled water and microwave-heated water. Although some reports say microwaved water is fine, others report negative results, claiming microwaved water destroys DNA and is not advised for infused waters and tea. Plus, if using a microwave, there is no way to watch the tiny bubbles that determine when your water is properly boiled. In fact, the water heated in a microwave never actually boils, but is still hotter than boiling water from a stovetop. I recommend boiling water in a stainless steel, porcelain, or glass pot, leaving its lid off. Boiling water in a traditional teakettle will not allow you to see at which boiling point to shut the heat off, although you could leave the lid off to see when the water starts to boil. Always start with room temperature filtered water before making tea or herbal infusions.

TEA BAGS VERSUS LOOSE TEA

What is the difference between a tea bag and loose tea? Loose tea may contain the leaf, stem, flower, and root. As such, loose tea can be a balance of all the parts of the plant, which gives it the total package of health benefits. Tea bags, when purchased from a reliable company, are very convenient. However, some companies may use powders and extracts in tea bags and the contents might be overprocessed. This is one reason to be sure the supplier or company you purchase your tea from practices high standards. Read ingredient labels, as some supermarket teas may contain artificial flavors and colorants.

Taste and quality varies among tea companies, and as you experiment, you will begin noticing the difference. You will also learn your preference for tea bags or loose tea, as well as for fresh versus dried loose tea. Fresh-from-the-garden herbs always make a delicious and very satisfying infusion.

ORGANIC VERSUS NONORGANIC

I highly recommend buying certified organic teas and herbal infusions. Pesticides, herbicides, and fertilizers found in nonorganic teas and herbal infusions are not a healthy choice for you or our planet. When plants are sprayed and forced to grow with chemicals, the quality of the plant is compromised. Chemicals and pesticides can cause eye and skin irritations and more serious diseases.

Be sure to do your due diligence when purchasing packages labeled "organic" or "natural," as some may be false advertising. To remind you to purchase from genuine organic sources, let me paint a little picture in your mind. Imagine placing an inorganic tea into your drinking water and letting it soak overnight, or placing it in hot water to extract the flavor. What you are extracting along with the flavor are chemical sprays and pesticides that might have been used on the plant. You're welcome!

It's easy to find organic high-quality tea from a reputable supplier, such as online or at a local tea store. The following are just some I found to be top-rated tea companies. Check their websites and see whether they appeal to you. Some of the teas may not be fair trade, but most of these companies seem to be true organic. From the food you eat to the beverages you drink, organic is the way to go.

Arbor Teas

Choice Organic Teas

Clipper Teas (UK and EU)

Firepot Nomadic Teas

Herbal Sage Tea Company

Level Ground (Colombia)

Mighty Leaf Tea

Mountain Rose Herbs

Numi Tea

Paromi Tea

Pukka Tea

Rishi Tea

Tea Leaf Company

Traditional Medicinals

Yogi Tea

Zhena's Gypsy Tea

Both organic unbleached tea bags and loose teas can be composted. Used tea leaves, worked into the soil, add nitrogen-rich components that balance out carbon-rich components.

INFUSERS

If not using tea bags, using infusers might be a good idea, as they are time savers for straining out the tea from your drinks. This is totally up to you, but tea infusers are pitchers or containers with a strainer in the middle that holds flowers, dried berries, and loose teas and herbs. The strainer keeps the infusion separated from the water, and allows for a longer infusion time while the bits of infusion stay away from your mouth or out of your cup or glass. Hot tea infusers have been around for a long time; the loose tea is placed in the mesh or pierced stainless steel ball or spoon and placed in a teapot or cup.

You can purchase organic, recyclable tea filter bags, reusable loose-leaf tea bags, stainless steel strainer spoons, or a variety of tea infusers online. There are all types of bleach-free, chemical-free, biodegradable, disposable empty tea bags you can fill with your favorite loose tea. They come in different shapes and make a beautiful presentation in a cup or glass. Any tea dealer will have several choices, or look online for a variety.

SWEETENERS

The less sugar we consume, the better our health. If you can do without sweetener in your infusions, all the better. If not, please use natural sweet fruits, pure maple syrup (or simple maple syrup; see page 168), coconut sugar, coconut nectar, stevia, or a dash of unsweetened fruit juice. For best health, do not use white sugar or artificial sweeteners. For additions to your cold brew infusions, you will find ice cube recipes made with fruit, flowers, juice, teas, and herbs, which can replace sweeteners (see page 171).

1. The quality and freshness of the tea used
2. The quantity of the tea used in proportion to the water
3. The quality of the water used
4. The cooling or boiling method
5. The length of time the tea steeps

Each recipe in this book suggests the amount of tea or herbs to use and a steeping time so you can start there and adjust to your liking. Experiment with longer or shorter steeping time as well as more or less tea to acquire your desired taste. Teas that are left in hot water too long can acquire a more bitter, tannic taste, whereas tea not steeped long enough can be too weak. Lower water temperatures work best with delicate green and white teas. Cold brew is always a safe bet.

You have read or heard about drinking green tea for our health, but there are other teas and herbal infusions you might not be aware of that can help boost your burn at the gym, help when you are feeling low energy or depressed, or help rid you of or prevent many diseases. You may become slimmer by drinking infused teas and herbal infusions instead of sugary drinks, get healthier from the teas' many benefits, and maybe even smile more because you feel so darn good. One thing is for sure: you will know you are getting the proper hydration and your skin will show it. Cold brew or hot infused water will be one of the easiest and healthiest things you can do for yourself.

GETTING STARTED

A woman is like a tea bag—you can't tell how strong she is until you put her in hot water.

—Eleanor Roosevelt

This book shares some of my favorite tea-, fruit-, and herbal-infused waters. You will enjoy drinking more water when it is infused with flavor. Many of these recipes combine teas, herbs, and fruits. Fruit infusions provide extra nutrients and health benefits. Once you get used to drinking tea and herbal infusions daily, you will understand the power and synergy of plants and water with your body.

What You Will Need

JAR SIZES AND MEASUREMENTS

Cold brew teas are easy to make using glass jars with a lid. Mason or Ball jars are convenient for making and storing cold brew teas. They are convenient for grab-and-go, and fun for parties. Having more infused liquid on hand will help you to drink more water and stay hydrated. A good reason to make larger batches of cold brew tea and herbal infusions is that you can then divide them into smaller jars and infuse them with different fruits or herbs. I've used a 24-ounce jar for most of these recipes. I make two or three jars at one time for variety throughout the day.

8-ounce jar = 1 cup
16-ounce jar = 2 cups
24-ounce jar = 3 cups
32-ounce jar = 4 cups
64-ounce jar = 8 cups

You will also need:
Organic tea bags or loose tea
Fresh or frozen fruit and herbs
Infuser (optional)
Ice cube trays

Cold Brew Infusion Basics

Cold brew teas are ideal infusions for hot days and summer parties. Cold brew infusions help us consume more water. They are simple to make and handy to have ready in the refrigerator to grab on the way to the gym or to work.

THE COLD BREW METHOD

The cold brew method uses time, not temperature, to extract the flavor and benefits of the infusion. Cold brew retains all the antioxidant benefits of the infusion, as it is not heated. Tea and herbal infusions have been around for centuries, but cold brew is a more recent style of preparation, which provides you with amazing taste and helps keep you well hydrated. Even if tea was never your thing, please try the cold brew method recipes. I'm confident you will become a fan.

Although hot tea is the most popular drink in the world next to water, some people don't care for tea, as the tannins—a slightly bitter-tasting substance in plant material—are too strong for their taste. Heat brings out the tannins, especially when tea is not brewed correctly. Some teas will have a bitter flavor if steeped too long, but when you cold brew the same tea, the flavor is smooth and refreshing. The first thing I noticed when I started drinking cold brew infusions daily was that my skin looked especially hydrated. What may be showing on the outside is doing something good on the inside. One of the reasons I'm excited to have you hop on the cold brew express train is that I'm personally benefiting from all the health benefits teas and herbal infusions provide, and I want you to enjoy the same experience.

I have a very busy schedule, and one of the nice things about cold brew infusions is the simplicity of the preparation. When making traditional iced tea, the water is boiled, cooled down, then chilled, but with cold brew all you do is add your ingredients to a container of filtered water, refrigerate for six hours or overnight, remove the tea, and that's it—your infusion is ready to drink! Add a bit of fruit or a splash of juice and hydration is easy.

One more method you might like for making cold brew tea is to place loose tea in a French coffee press. Add filtered water and let brew in the refrigerator overnight. In the morning, just press down the handle and pour the silky-smooth liquid into a lidded glass container. No straining necessary. What could be easier?

When making cold brew refrigerator infusions, use high-quality organic tea bags or loose tea. Reliable tea companies have many of their own special blends available both loose and in bags. Purchase any flavor combinations that appeal to you and ask about the health properties of the teas you choose. Brewing time is six hours to overnight.

The slower extraction of cold brew teas produces a flavorful infusion and there is little concern of oversteeping or bitterness if you leave the bags in longer. You can mix and match your favorite teas together to create your own special blend. I can't say enough about this easy, delicious method. Cold brews keep best for two to three days in the refrigerator.

TIP: For a quicker cold brewing time, add one more tea bag or teaspoon of loose tea than the recipe calls for. Taste in five hours to see whether the tea is to your liking. If so, remove the bags and enjoy. I like to call it overnight tea as I prefer the taste of a longer brewing time, but sometimes I just can't wait and drink it after a few hours of brewing. Keep some of these cold brew teas in handy 8-ounce jars in your refrigerator to grab on your way out the door and to give the kids a healthy drink.

HOW TO MAKE COLD BREW TEA AND HERBAL INFUSIONS

- Use 3 or 4 tea bags for a 24-ounce jar.
- Use 5 to 6 tea bags for a 32-ounce (quart-size) jar.
- Use 10 to 12 bags for a 64-ounce (2-quart) jar.

Although one tea bag usually contains 1 teaspoon of tea, I like using 1 tablespoon of loose tea per 8 ounces of water.

Fill the container with filtered water. Drop in the tea bags and let the strings hang over the top of the jar. Put on the lid and refrigerate. If using loose tea, drop right into the jar or use a tea infuser (see page 26). Refrigerate for 6 hours or overnight. Make cold brew tea at night and it's ready in the morning to grab and go.

Taste and see whether the infusion is to your liking. When ready, remove the bags or strain out the loose tea. This is the time to add fruit or herbs for a further infusion.

COLD BREW LATTE

I love, love, love cold brew lattes. For an afternoon pick-me-up or a morning treat, a cold brew latte really does the trick.

INGREDIENTS

8 ounces cold brew tea or herbal infusion

⅛ to ¼ cup nondairy milk, such as almond milk or coconut milk

A dash of pure maple syrup or your sweetener of choice (see page 26), to taste

METHOD

Stir the ingredients well in a glass, or for a yummy frozen version, combine the tea, milk, and sweetener in a blender, toss in three or four ice cubes, and blitz until frosty. Pour into a glass and enjoy.

NOTE: If you live in cold weather a majority of the year, don't think that cold brew tea is out of the question for you. Make the cold brew tea recipes, and they will be in your refrigerator ready to warm up when needed. Do not boil; just warm in a pan over low heat to your liking. Having cold brew in your refrigerator will make it easier for you to remember to stay hydrated. Even on a cold morning, it's a welcoming sight to have a brew ready to quickly warm up. Make a warm latte and I know you will be very happy to enjoy this treat.

DECOCTION INFUSION

A decoction is an herbal tea preparation made by simmering hard roots, barks, berries, and seeds in water for a period of time. A decoction draws out and releases the hard plant matter. This liquid can be stored in a glass jar in the refrigerator for 48 hours. Ginger, chicory, echinacea, astragalus, fennel, burdock, and turmeric are popular ingredients used for decoctions. Cardamom seeds, cinnamon bark, and dried berries, such as hawthorn, are also good material for decoctions. Decoctions are used by the spoonful in tea or herbal waters. They are a good way to extract the most from the roots and hard plant matter.

INGREDIENTS

2 tablespoons dried herbs or spices per cup of room temperature filtered water (if using fresh herbs, double or triple the amount)

24 ounces filtered water, at room temperature

Sweetener (see page 26; optional)

METHOD

Place the plant matter and water in a nonreactive pot with a lid. Over low heat, slowly bring the water to a simmer and cover. Gently simmer for 20 to 40 minutes. The water will evaporate slightly. Turn off the heat, allow to cool for 5 minutes, then strain the herbs over a bowl. Using a second bowl, pour the liquid back over the herbs in the strainer. Place the liquid in a lidded jar and store in the refrigerator for 3 to 4 days.

Some decoction infusions might require a sweetener for enjoyment; if so, use healthy options. To use, add decoctions by the spoonful to water for cold brew or hot tea.

NOTE: Decoctions can be frozen in ice cube trays.

Hot Water Tea and Herbal Infusions

Most people are familiar with hot tea. Heat water, drop in a tea bag, and steep. Add milk, sweetener, or lemon, and you have a cup of tea. Hot infusions draw out the aromatic oils from the herbs. On a cold day, there is nothing better to warm you up and help fulfill your water needs. If you are weaning yourself off coffee, the right hot teas can do the trick.

Many people forget to consume water on cold days, but just because the weather is chilly it doesn't mean you don't need hydration. Of course, you need more water during summer months, but hot teas hydrate you and they are very soothing. If someone is sick, a hot tea can be a comforting drink. If you need a pick-me-up in cold weather, hot herbal teas are a great choice.

Just about any tea can be made into a cold brew, but some teas lend themselves to soothing hot tea or herbal infusions. Drinking four or five cups of hot tea or herbal infusions daily can give your health a boost. Hot tea and hot herbal infusions have their place for attaining good health, and there is nothing like a hot tea on a cold day to make you feel all cozy inside.

If you get hooked on cold brew tea, see the basic instructions on page 31 for making any of these hot infusion recipes in this book into a cold brew. When brewing loose-leaf hot teas, a tea infuser is very convenient and saves time spent straining. Just lift out the tea infuser and your tea is ready to drink. A French press coffee maker is another great way to make hot teas.

Although I call these hot teas, the water should not boil rapidly; lightly simmered water is best as very hot water extracts more tannin from the tea and can make your drink bitter. Also, steeping too long can make a tea bitter, so be sure to read the directions for each tea recipe, as steeping times may differ. In the end, use your own taste buds, tea by tea, to determine what steeping time tastes best to you.

COLD BREW TRUE TEAS

I mention true teas throughout the book as they are considered the only "real" tea. Black, green, oolong, and white tea fall into this category. Many people think herbal blends are tea as well, but they are not considered tea in the world of teas. *Herbal infusions* is the proper name for those. *True tea* is the term given to the four teas that come from the same plant, *Camellia sinensis*. You will find many recipes here made with true teas.

The difference between true tea colors pertains to fermentation or oxidation that occurs naturally in the leaves and changes their color and flavor. The leaves are rolled and the surface of the leaf is cracked so oxygen will react with the plant's enzymes. Black tea is fully oxidized, oolong tea is partially oxidized, and green and white teas are not oxidized, which makes them lighter in taste and aroma. Drinking tea supports detoxification of the body. Cold brew or hot, with a squeeze of citrus or fruit infusions, these drinks can revitalize your cells.

True teas contain differing levels of caffeine and are considered medicinal teas. They combine well with any herbal teas to make a brew.

NOTE: Although these recipes specify using black, oolong, green, or white tea, any true tea may be substituted.

Black tea gets its name from the leaves, which are exposed to oxygen; this turns the leaves black. Black tea contains larger amounts of caffeine than the other true teas. As such, it can be a good coffee replacer in the morning. Black tea's health benefits outweigh those of coffee, as black tea helps promote blood flow in the brain without causing pressure to the heart. Black tea is high in antioxidants, has soothing anti-inflammatory effects on the digestive tract, and may help protect arteries from clogging. Black tea may help open breathing channels, control cholesterol, aid digestion, and can have a blood sugar–lowering effect for diabetics. It's also known for reducing the risk of heart disease. Just as with green tea, four or five cups a day is recommended.

NOTE: If you have an allergy to caffeine, drink herbal infusions instead.

DARJEELING COLD BREW TEA + ORANGE SLICES

Darjeeling is a tea from the Darjeeling district in West Bengal, India. It is available in black, oolong, green, and white. When brewed, it produces a light-colored, thin-bodied infusion with a floral aroma.

INGREDIENTS

24 ounces filtered water

3 to 4 Darjeeling tea bags, or 2 tablespoons loose tea

3 orange slices, rinds removed

METHOD

Place the water and tea bags or loose tea in a lidded mason jar, cover, and refrigerate for 5 hours, then place the orange slices in the jar. Further infuse the tea for another hour or overnight. Remove the bags or strain out the loose tea when the tea is to your liking.

DARJEELING TEA

Like all teas, Darjeeling possesses beneficial catechins and flavonoids; it also helps improve oral health, promotes strong bones, and is good for heart health, weight loss, and digestion.

BLACK COLD BREW TEA + BLACKBERRIES

Pairing blackberries with black tea adds a sweet taste and extra nutrients. This brew makes a great latte: just add any nondairy milk to the already sweetened tea.

INGREDIENTS

24 ounces filtered water

3 to 4 black tea bags, or 2 tablespoons loose tea

¼ to ½ cup chopped blackberries

Infused ice cubes (see page 171; optional)

METHOD

Place the water and tea bags or loose tea in a lidded mason jar, cover, and refrigerate for 4 to 6 hours or overnight, adding the blackberries halfway through brewing. Remove the bags or strain out the loose tea. Eat the blackberries or leave in for a further infusion.

Add infused ice cubes as a sweetener, if desired, when serving.

ORANGE COLD BREW TEA + VANILLA BEAN + RASPBERRIES

In the tea industry, tea leaves are graded on the quality and condition of the leaves. The highest grades are referred to as orange pekoe. However, the term has nothing to do with oranges; it is simply a grade of black tea. This recipe is made with oranges and black tea. Oranges contain a high amount of vitamin C and raspberries are loaded with antioxidants. This cold brew tea contains an abundance of health benefits.

INGREDIENTS

24 ounces filtered water

3 black tea bags, or 1½ heaping tablespoons loose tea

⅛ cup dried orange slices (see page 168)

One 1-inch piece vanilla bean

ADD-INS

¼ cup fresh or frozen raspberries

METHOD

Place the water, tea bags or loose tea, dried orange, and vanilla bean in a lidded mason jar and refrigerate for 6 hours or overnight. When tea is ready to your taste, remove the bags or strain out the loose tea. Remove the orange and vanilla bean, or leave them in if you would like a stronger infusion. At this time it's best to remove the rind from the orange and place the fruit back in the container if you are further infusing. Removing the rind prevents any bitterness.

TO FURTHER INFUSE: Add fresh or frozen raspberries.

BLACK COLD BREW TEA + LEMON + POMEGRANATE JUICE

Surrender to the taste of black tea laced with lemon and pomegranate juice. Pomegranate juice is loaded with antioxidants and gives this tea a soft, sweet taste.

INGREDIENTS

24 ounces filtered water

3 to 4 black tea bags, or 2 tablespoons loose tea

ADD-INS

2 lemon slices

2 tablespoons pomegranate juice (see page 145 to make your own)

Infused ice cubes (see page 171; optional)

METHOD

Place the water and tea bags or loose tea in a lidded mason jar, cover, and refrigerate. Taste after 5 hours and, if it is to your liking, remove the bags or strain out the loose tea. If it needs more time, check again in 1 to 2 more hours.

TO FURTHER INFUSE: Add the lemon slices and pomegranate juice, plus infused ice cubes, if desired.

SUN BREW TEA

I've been making sun tea since the early 1970s. You could always find a few jars steeping on our patio. My house was the hangout for my children's friends, and even in the early days, I thought sugary drinks were not healthy, so sun tea was always available in our home. Use a lidded glass jar for making sun tea, as plastic chemicals can leech into the water. This is especially true when the container is in the sun.

INGREDIENTS

Filtered water (for a 2-gallon jar, use 8 tea bags; for a 1-gallon jar, use 4 tea bags; for loose tea, use 1 heaping teaspoon per 8 ounces of water)

ADD-INS (OPTIONAL)

Chopped or sliced apple, orange, strawberries, lemon, or other fruit

Sweetener (see page 26)

METHOD

Fill a jar with filtered water. If using tea bags, set the tea bags inside and let the strings hang over the top of the jar. Put on the lid to hold the tea bags in place. If using loose tea, add to the water.

Place the jar in the sun to steep for 4 to 6 hours.

Bring the jar inside. Squeeze out and remove the bags or strain out the loose tea.

TO FURTHER INFUSE: Add chopped or sliced apple, orange, strawberries, lemon, or other fruit to the sun-brewed tea, then place in the refrigerator to infuse for 2 to 4 hours or longer.

If sweetener is desired, add to each serving, not to the whole jar.

NOTE: The Centers for Disease Control (CDC) claims bacteria may form in sun tea. I've never had this problem in all my years of making sun tea, but if a film forms on top of the tea, that means bacteria has bloomed, so I would advise you to dump it out.

Falling between green and black teas is oolong, with its partially oxidized leaves. Oolong provides the benefits of both black and green teas, and has a fruity flavor. Oolong tea leaves are high in polyphenols and antioxidants. Oolong is often the tea of choice for weight control and is known to help alleviate skin conditions. The USDA Agricultural Research Service's Diet, Genomics, and Immunology Laboratory claims that people who drink four or more cups of oolong tea daily burn 67 more calories per day than do people who drink water. Oolong is a metabolism-boosting tea, and is good for heart health. It fights inflammation, supports healthy brain function, prevents bone mass loss, and may help prevent diabetes. A word of caution: Oolong tea does contain caffeine, so if you are sensitive to caffeine, drink oolong in moderation or go with herbal infusions instead.

OOLONG COLD BREW TEA + BERRIES OR STONE FRUIT

Oolong tea is the tea I remember from my childhood. When eating at an Asian restaurant, my mother loved this hot tea that was served in a small ceramic teapot along with tiny cups without handles. As much as she enjoyed this tea, we never had it at home—the only tea I remember there was Lipton. In my early years, I didn't know teas had health properties; I just thought anything I could put sugar in was a treat. Now, I avoid sugars and enjoy the health benefits of this tea and its natural taste.

INGREDIENTS

24 ounces filtered water

3 oolong tea bags, or 1½ tablespoons loose tea

ADD-INS

¼ to ½ cup fresh or frozen berries or sliced mango, peach, or nectarine

METHOD

Place the water and tea bags or loose tea in lidded mason jar, cover, and refrigerate for 4 to 6 hours or overnight. Remove the bags or strain out the loose tea.

TO FURTHER INFUSE: Add fresh or frozen berries or sliced mango, peach, or nectarine.

OOLONG COLD BREW TEA + COCONUT MILK

Enhance the sweet taste of oolong tea by adding coconut milk for a creamy texture. All the goodness and health benefits of both tea and milk will certainly delight your taste buds. Toss some ice in your glass when ready to drink and enjoy a lovely healthy treat. Add sweetener, if desired.

INGREDIENTS

24 ounces filtered water

3 oolong tea bags, or 1½ tablespoons loose tea

ADD-INS

⅛ to ¼ cup coconut milk

Sweetener (see page 26; optional)

METHOD

Place the water and tea bags or loose tea in a lidded mason jar, cover, and refrigerate for 4 to 6 hours or overnight. Remove the bags or strain out the loose tea. To serve, add the coconut milk and sweetener, if desired. For a frosty drink, freeze coconut milk in ice trays and then blend until icy. Spoon into individual servings.

GREEN TEA

Perhaps the best known of the four true teas, green tea has been used as a health cure for centuries. Originating in China, Japan, and India, it is now grown around the world. Extremely high in antioxidants, it contains vitamins A, C, E, F, P, U, and thiamine (an amino acid); chlorophyll; and powerful polyphenols. Some of the healing properties attributed to green tea include helping prevent plaque and cavities, and helping to slow down the aging process. Green tea burns fat, lowers blood pressure and blood sugar, fights free radicals, and strengthens the immune system. Epigallocatechin gallate (EGCG), a health-boosting antioxidant found in green tea, is said to help the body in many ways. Because of its high antioxidant content, green tea has a positive effect on healthy cell growth. Green tea helps reduce bad cholesterol and although it contains caffeine, which boosts metabolism and aids in weight loss, it may also have a component that relaxes and calms the body. More studies have been done on green tea than other teas, and the research continues to discover the possible effects of green tea on preventing certain cancers.

GREEN COLD BREW TEA + BLUEBERRIES OR STONE FRUIT

Green tea has a milder flavor than black tea but can be made the same basic way with a different fruit infusion. Try a green tea latte as a pick-me-up between breakfast and lunch.

INGREDIENTS

24 ounces filtered water

3 green tea bags, or 1½ tablespoons loose tea

ADD-INS

¼ to ½ cup blueberries or sliced stone fruit, such as peaches or nectarine

Infused ice cubes (optional; see page 171)

METHOD

Place the water and tea bags or loose tea in a lidded mason jar, cover, and refrigerate for 4 to 6 hours or overnight. Remove the bags or strain out the loose tea.

TO FURTHER INFUSE: Add blueberries or stone fruit and infused ice cubes, if using, to sweeten.

GREEN COLD BREW TEA + LAVENDER + LEMON

This combination is as light and delicious as a drink can be, but it also has many health benefits. Did you know that lavender has the ability to relieve stress? It can also improve your mood and help with skin irritations, is anti-inflammatory, and soothes stomach bloating. It's good to know you can get all this goodness in one tea drink. But wait, there's more: add some lemon, which is high in vitamin C and potassium, and give your immune system a boost. Lemon alkalizes and detoxifies, so drink up!

INGREDIENTS

24 ounces filtered water

3 green tea bags, or 1½ tablespoons loose tea

1 teaspoon culinary lavender buds (here's where it's nice to use an infuser)

2 lemon slices to infuse, plus more for serving

1 teaspoon fresh lemon juice

Infused ice cubes (see page 171)

METHOD

Place the water and tea bags or loose tea in a lidded mason jar and add the lavender, lemon slices, and lemon juice. Cover and refrigerate for 6 hours or overnight. Remove the bags or strain out the loose tea, and strain out the lemon slices and lavender. Serve in a glass with infused ice cubes and garnish with fresh sliced lemon.

GREEN COLD BREW TEA + LEMON

Lemonade meets iced tea in this recipe.

INGREDIENTS

24 ounces filtered water

3 green or white tea bags or 1½ tablespoons loose green or white tea

5 or 6 lemon slices, rinds removed

Lemon-infused ice cubes (see page 171; optional)

METHOD

Place the water, tea bags or loose tea, and lemon slices in a lidded mason jar, cover, and refrigerate for 6 hours or overnight. Remove the bags and lemon slices, or strain the liquid if using loose tea. Add lemon-infused ice cubes, if desired.

GREEN COLD BREW TEA + MANGO + COCONUT WATER

This exotic combination of green tea, mango, and coconut water has numerous health benefits. Mango has antioxidant compounds as well as quercetin, isoquercitrin, astragalin, fisetin, gallic acid, and methylgallat, and an abundance of enzymes. You will have done yourself a great favor by drinking this brew. Plus, coconut water is high in potassium and electrolytes. Just think how hydrating this will be for you!

INGREDIENTS

24 ounces filtered water

3 green mint tea bags, or 2 green tea and 1 mint tea bag, or 1 tablespoon of loose green tea and 1 sprig fresh mint

ADD-INS

¼ to ½ cup fresh or frozen mango chunks or slices

¼ to ½ cup coconut water

Infused ice cubes (see page 171)

Mint sprig for serving

METHOD

Place the water, tea bags or loose tea, and mint, if using, in a lidded mason jar, cover, and refrigerate for 6 hours or overnight. Remove the bags or strain out the loose tea.

TO FURTHER INFUSE: Add mango chunks or slices and coconut water. Serve over infused ice cubes and garnish with a mint sprig.

GREEN COLD BREW TEA + MINT + LIME

Add a hint of mint and some citrus in the form of lime, and both the taste and healthy properties of your green tea will be enhanced.

INGREDIENTS

24 ounces filtered water

3 green tea bags, or 1½ tablespoons loose tea

1 sprig fresh mint

ADD-INS

1 sprig fresh mint

2 lime slices

METHOD

Place the water, tea bags or loose tea, and mint sprig in a lidded mason jar, cover, and refrigerate overnight. Remove the bags and mint, or strain the liquid if using loose tea. To serve, add the additional mint and the lime slices.

JASMINE COLD BREW TEA +
INFUSED ICE CUBES

Aromatic jasmine tea is sweet and mellow, its fragrance light and unique. Both the blossoms and leaves are used to extract the essence. Commonly, jasmine tea has a base of white or green tea, which is scented with this essence by means of complex air filtering. The aroma and lightness of the tea is wonderful enjoyed without additional flavoring, but feel free to serve with infused ice cubes (see page 171) or a squeeze of lemon juice as a special treat. Jasmine makes a lovely warm brew as well.

INGREDIENTS

24 ounces filtered water

2 jasmine tea bags, or 1½ tablespoons loose tea

1 green tea bag, or 1 tablespoon loose tea

Infused ice cubes (see page 171)

METHOD

Place the water and tea bags or loose tea in a lidded mason jar, cover, and refrigerate for 6 hours or overnight. Remove the bags or strain out the loose tea. Serve with infused ice cubes.

JASMINE TEA

Jasmine tea has been used for centuries in Asia for its health benefits, including easing inflammation, reducing the risk of heart attack, building a stronger immune system, reducing pain, aiding weight loss, helping control diabetes, lowering cholesterol, helping with digestion, and eliminating bacteria. Jasmine tea also contains antioxidants, such as catechins and epicatechins, which have a wide range of benefits to the body. Jasmine infusions are known to be calming.

To fully enjoy, purchase the best quality pure loose jasmine tea from a reputable dealer.

MOROCCAN MINT GREEN COLD BREW TEA + BERRIES + LEMON SLICES

In Morocco, where the summers are scorching, people drink hot Moroccan mint tea all summer long to cool down. People increase the amount they sweat when they drink a hot beverage, and the evaporation of that sweat releases body heat. Moroccan mint tea helps soothe an upset stomach, relieves heartburn, boosts mental performance, promotes focus, loosens congestion, alleviates nasal allergies, clears skin disorders, and keeps your breath fresh. Mint is very easy to grow and spreads so quickly it can take over your garden; it can be grown in pots or in a small space, if necessary. In Morocco, India, Argentina, Thailand, Taiwan, and other countries, hot mint tea is served in a glass, not a mug, so my cold brew Moroccan mint recipe fits nicely into an international scene. Spearmint supports good digestion, circulation, stress relief, and strengthens the immune system.

INGREDIENTS

24 ounces filtered water

2 Moroccan mint green tea bags or 1½ tablespoons loose tea

1 spearmint tea bag or 1 tablespoon loose tea

ADD-INS

1 small handful berries (optional)

2 lemon slices

1 sprig fresh spearmint for serving

METHOD

Place the water and tea bags or loose tea in a lidded mason jar. If using bags, let the strings hang over the top of the jar. Cover and refrigerate for 6 hours or, better, overnight. Remove the bags or strain out the loose tea.

TO FURTHER INFUSE: Add a small handful of berries for extra sweetness, if desired, lemon slices, and fresh mint sprigs

MOROCCAN MINT

Consuming Moroccan mint tea regularly alerts and energizes the brain cells to work more attentively. Moroccan mint, paired with green tea, has been used for centuries in traditional Chinese and Ayurvedic medicine to help with digestion, support heart health, and stabilize blood sugar. This ancient tradition has thousands of studies indicating that green tea contains antioxidants that are more powerful than vitamin C, as well as other substances that help control cholesterol and heart disease and assist with many other health concerns.

ROOIBOS AND GREEN COLD BREW TEA + RASPBERRIES + PEACHES

Caffeine-free rooibos is native to South Africa. It is amazingly delicious and healthy on its own, even without green tea being added, and is a staple in my refrigerator. Rooibos makes a delicious latte or cozy hot tea as well. Although rooibos contains no caffeine, green tea does, so it is best to drink this blend in the early part of the day.

INGREDIENTS

24 ounces filtered water

2 rooibos tea bags, or 2 heaping teaspoons loose rooibos tea

1 green tea bag or 1 heaping teaspoon loose green tea

ADD-INS

6 to 8 raspberries

3 fresh or frozen peach slices

METHOD

Place the water and tea bags or loose tea in a lidded mason jar. If using bags, let the string hang over the top of the jar. Cover and refrigerate for 6 hours or overnight. Remove the bags or strain out the loose tea.

TO FURTHER INFUSE: Add raspberries and peach slices.

ROOIBOS TEA

Rooibos tea contains minerals, including iron, calcium, potassium, and zinc. Studies show that rooibos also has 37 natural antioxidants, which help fight disease. An infusion aids in stress release, helps maintain healthy teeth and bones, relieves stomach and digestive discomforts, and is known to help increase iron absorption. Rooibos may cure a headache, help you sleep better, and is good for asthma relief and eczema. Claims have been made that rooibos infusion may help lower blood pressure and slow loss of bone mass, allergies, and premature aging. This infusion can relieve cramps and boost the immune system. Mixing rooibos with green tea supplies you with a tasty, powerful mixture.

WHITE TEA

White tea is harvested only a few days each spring. They are baby tea leaves, harvested by hand from the tip of the plant. They undergo virtually no processing; have the least amount of caffeine compared to green, oolong, and black teas; and boast high antioxidant properties. White tea is considered to be one of the healthiest of teas and makes a lovely hot tea as well.

It is claimed that white tea extract breaks down fat in human cells. But drinking white tea daily won't replace diet and exercise, so don't just sit at your desk all day sipping white tea and expecting the scale to give you good news. White tea may be helpful for cardiovascular disorders, lowering blood pressure, and antiaging. It can help protect the skin from harmful UV rays (though it's not a replacement for sunscreen) and has antibacterial properties.

White tea is a good mix with herbal infusions: the caffeine is lessened and the benefits of herbal and white tea are plentiful. In spite of its name, when brewed it turns a light yellow.

CHAI AND WHITE COLD BREW TEA + ORANGE SLICES

Chai is a popular drink in India and used for health and peace of mind. It balances the immune system, improves digestion, fights inflammation, and is loaded with antioxidants. Chai is a blend of tea, herbs, and spices, including black tea, ginger, cardamom, cinnamon, cloves, fennel, and black pepper. Each of these ingredients has health benefits of its own and together they become a powerful mixture that excites the taste buds. When cold brewed, the taste is smooth and mild.

Buy the best-quality chai you can find, as its taste and quality vary widely. Masala chai is black tea mixed with herbs and spices. In India, it is prepared with milk. Almond or other nondairy milk smoothes the strong taste; add a little sweetener and masala chai makes a nice morning latte. Here, we mix chai with white tea. Delicious cold brewed or hot, this might end up being one of your favorite morning drinks.

INGREDIENTS

24 ounces filtered water

2 chai bags or 1 tablespoon chai, 1 white tea bag,
or ½ tablespoon white loose tea

ADD-INS (PER SERVING)

⅛ cup nondairy milk

1 to 2 orange slices

METHOD

Place the water and tea bags or loose tea in a lidded mason jar. If using bags, let the strings hang over the top of the jar. Cover and refrigerate for 6 hours or overnight. Remove the bags or strain out the loose tea.

TO SERVE: Add nondairy milk and a slice or two of orange or squeeze in the juice from one orange slice.

CHAI

Chai means "tea" in Hindi (the primary language spoken in northern India), so if you say "chai tea," which is a term used in the United States, you are actually saying "tea tea." When ordering chai in a coffee shop, be sure there is no sugar added. Chai lattes in coffee shops are usually made with a powdered mixture that contains white sugar. It may taste good, but is not the same as healthy unsweetened chai. It's best to ask for a tea bag and hot water, not a latte, with a side of almond or other nondairy milk, and add your own healthier sweetener.

WHITE COLD BREW TEA + BERRIES OR STONE FRUIT

Like green, oolong, and black tea, white tea is good to use as a base for many infusions in place of plain water. Once this tea is made, you can divide it into smaller jars for a variety of fruit infusions.

INGREDIENTS

24 ounces filtered water

1 or 2 white tea bags, or 1 to 2 tablespoons loose tea

ADD-INS

¼ to ½ cup fresh or frozen berries, mango, peach, or nectarine

Infused ice cubes (see page 171)

METHOD

Place the water and tea bags or loose tea in a lidded mason jar, cover, and refrigerate for 4 to 6 hours or overnight. Remove the bags or strain out the loose tea.

TO FURTHER INFUSE: Divide among smaller jars, if you wish. Add fresh or frozen berries, mango, peach, or nectarine. To serve, add infused ice cubes as a sweetener.

WHITE AND ROOIBOS COLD BREW TEA + VANILLA BEAN + STRAWBERRIES

White tea has a small amount of caffeine and rooibos is caffeine-free. This combination has the benefits of two very powerful teas, and sends a message to your body that it is in good hands. See for yourself how this cold brew makes you feel. If it does for you what it does for me, you will be going back many times for more.

INGREDIENTS

24 ounces filtered water

2 white tea bags, or 1 tablespoon loose tea

1 rooibos tea bag, or 2 teaspoons loose tea

One 2-inch piece vanilla bean

ADD-INS

¼ cup hulled strawberries

METHOD

Place the water, tea bags or loose tea, and vanilla bean in a lidded mason jar. If using bags, let the strings hang over the top of the jar. Cover and refrigerate for 6 hours or overnight. Remove the bags or strain out the loose tea, and remove the vanilla bean.

TO FURTHER INFUSE: Add strawberries.

COLD BREW HERBAL INFUSIONS

Although many people call all herbal plant matter tea, the true teas—black, oolong, green, and white—are the only real teas, which come from the same plant, the *Camellia sinensis*. In the tea world, herbal infusions are not called tea. Any leaf, plant, flower, root, or fruit that does not come from the *C. sinensis* plant is known as an herbal infusion. This is an important difference as the health benefits, flavor, and nutritional value vary in herbal plants. By blending a number of these herbal elements together, special infusions can be made. However, mixing true tea and herbal infusions is commonplace.

Unlike true teas, herbal infusions are caffeine-free. Most herbal infusions may be safe in small quantities for pregnant women and children. If you are pregnant or nursing, always check with your doctor before adding teas or herbal infusions to your diet. Herbal infusions are high in minerals and can support a healthy immune system. They are a good fighter of colds and flu, and may help alleviate sleep problems. Herbs can lessen cramps, aid digestion, and help with detoxification and weight loss.

CHAMOMILE COLD BREW INFUSION + APPLE + ORANGE

Nothing wrong with a chamomile infusion on its own, but adding apples and oranges sweetens the flavor and gives you added nutrients when you consume the fruit. This is a delicious soothing infusion to brighten and defuse a stressful day. Chamomile makes a nice warm drink as well, but sipping a cool chamomile cold brew on a summer evening is the perfect relaxer.

INGREDIENTS

24 ounces filtered water

3 chamomile tea bags, or 1½ tablespoons loose tea

¼ to ½ apple, thinly sliced

¼ to ½ orange, thinly sliced

METHOD

Place the water, tea bags or loose tea, and fruit in a lidded mason jar, cover, and refrigerate for 6 hours or overnight. Remove the bags or strain out the loose tea. Taste to see whether the infusion is to your liking. If so, you can eat the apple and orange slices or leave them in for a longer time. Citrus rinds can be bitter, so cut the rind off the orange before continuing to infuse.

CHAMOMILE

Chamomile is known to be relaxing; it can help in fighting depression and anxiety, muscle spasms, and allergies. Chamomile can also relieve insomnia and skin disorders as well as help with arthritis pain and gastrointestinal disorders. It is anti-inflammatory, high in antioxidants, and fights free radical damage. In addition, chamomile tea is antiaging.

HIBISCUS COLD BREW INFUSION + PINEAPPLE + CRANBERRY JUICE

A hibiscus infusion is delicious and beautiful. Its reddish color and medicinal properties make this a perfect drink. Pineapple is good for immunity support, bone strength, and eye health. Cranberry juice can help with urinary tract infections and the berries are packed with nutrients that help ward off infections. This trifecta might be the drink for you.

INGREDIENTS

24 ounces filtered water

3 hibiscus tea bags, or 1½ tablespoons loose tea

ADD-INS

¼ cup fresh or frozen pineapple, or 1 tablespoon pineapple juice

1 tablespoon cranberry juice

1 orange slice for serving

1 cinnamon stick for serving

METHOD

Place the water and tea bags or loose tea in a lidded mason jar, cover, and refrigerate for 6 hours or overnight. Remove the bags or strain out the loose tea.

TO FURTHER INFUSE: Add fresh or frozen pineapple or pineapple juice along with the cranberry juice. Garnish with an orange slice and a cinnamon stick.

CHAMOMILE COLD BREW INFUSION + LEMONGRASS

Just one cup of this soothing, low-calorie, and low cholesterol–promoting tea may improve your health in many ways. I prefer my chamomile loose, as the dried daisy-looking flowers of chamomile infusion are quite beautiful to look at. This infusion should be in any tea lover's collection.

INGREDIENTS

24 ounces filtered water

3 chamomile tea bags, or 1½ tablespoons loose tea

One 3-inch piece fresh lemongrass, or 2 teaspoons loose lemon balm leaves

2 lemon slices, rind removed, to infuse, plus more intact lemon slices for serving

Infused ice cubes (page 171; optional)

METHOD

Place the water, tea bags or loose tea, lemongrass, and lemon slices in a lidded mason jar, cover, and refrigerate overnight. Remove the bags or strain out the loose tea. Strain out and discard the infused lemongrass and lemon. Add fresh lemon slices. Serve in a glass with infused ice cubes or drink straight from the jar.

HOPS, KAVA, OR SKULLCAP COLD BREW INFUSION + BERRIES

Any of these three herbs is good for relaxation and relieving stress and anxiety. You can make a light cold brew to sip throughout the day, especially if you expect an extra-stressful workday or evening event. Sipping this infusion won't knock you out, but you might like the meditative feeling it gives you. Feel free to mix and match the fruit, or use more fruit if you desire.

CAUTION: Because hops, kava, and skullcap can have sedative effects, check with your health-care professional before consuming these infusions.

INGREDIENTS

24 ounces filtered water

3 hops, kava, or skullcap tea bags, or 1½ tablespoons loose tea

ADD-INS

½ cup blueberries, raspberries, or strawberries

Infused ice cubes (see page 171)

METHOD

Place the water and tea bags or loose tea in a lidded mason jar, cover, and refrigerate overnight. Remove the bags or strain out the loose tea.

TO FURTHER INFUSE: Place blueberries, raspberries, or strawberries in the jar and muddle a bit to release some of the juices. To serve, pour into a glass or 8-ounce jar and add infused ice cubes.

HOPS, KAVA, AND SKULLCAP

Hops, kava, and skullcap are all good for insomnia and have anti-inflammatory effects. They are also high in antioxidants and are antimicrobial.

LADY'S MANTLE COLD BREW INFUSION + LEMON + RASPBERRIES

European women have been using lady's mantle tea for centuries. It is caffeine-free and can make a hot or cold brew. Check Amazon or other online sites to purchase this herb, or grow and dry it yourself.

INGREDIENTS

24 ounces filtered water

3 lady's mantle tea bags, or ½ cup fresh lady's mantle leaves, or 1½ tablespoons dried

1 teaspoon lemon balm leaves, or 2 lemon slices

ADD-INS

¼ cup fresh or frozen raspberries

Infused ice cubes (see page 171)

METHOD

Place the water, tea bag or loose leaves, and lemon balm or lemon slices in a lidded mason jar, cover, and refrigerate for 6 hours or overnight. Remove the bags or strain out the leaves (or lemon slices, if using).

TO FURTHER INFUSE: Add fresh or frozen raspberries and infuse for 3 to 4 more hours. Pour into a glass and add infused ice cubes for a refreshing, beneficial drink.

LADY'S MANTLE

There are more than 300 varieties of lady's mantle in Europe. It was mainly used for relieving menstrual cramps (begin drinking the tea about a week before you are expecting your period), but its medicinal properties are many. Lady's mantle can relieve sore throats, reduce inflammation, and promote weight loss. Just like so many other herbal teas, lady's mantle is high in antioxidants, which are known to slow down the aging process. You can enjoy younger-looking skin because the antioxidants fight off free radicals that accelerate aging. This infusion is also good for skin issues, such as eczema and rashes. Try washing your hair with lady's mantle, as it can make your hair healthy and shiny.

MINT COLD BREW INFUSION + BLACKBERRIES

Mint is very refreshing and has many positive effects on your health. This recipe adds sweet and juicy blackberries, which, with their rich, dark purple color, are loaded with antioxidants. You might be surprised to learn that blackberries contain protein and vitamins A, C, and E. They also contain potassium, copper, iron, magnesium, and zinc. Eat the berries after they infuse your water, for their full benefits.

INGREDIENTS

24 ounces filtered water

2 mint tea bags, ½ cup fresh mint leaves, or 1 tablespoon dried mint

ADD-INS

½ cup blackberries

Infused ice cubes (page 171; optional)

1 sprig mint for serving (optional)

METHOD

Place the water and tea bags or loose leaves in a lidded mason jar, cover, and refrigerate overnight. Remove the bags or strain out the leaves.

TO FURTHER INFUSE: Add blackberries to the jar and muddle with a wooden spoon to release some of the juices, or add a few fresh blackberries to your serving glass with some infused ice cubes and a sprig of mint to garnish.

MINT

Mint is recommended for digestion, nausea, asthma, headaches, and weight loss, and is being studied for cancer prevention. In addition, mint promotes eye health and brain function, reduces inflammation, and boosts immunity. This herb is very easy to grow and does well in pots.

MINT COLD BREW INFUSION + STRAWBERRIES

Mint is an impressive herb. Its taste and smell are delicious and its health properties are abundant. The strawberries in this drink provide a high antioxidant boost. Strawberries are treated with more pesticides and chemicals than any other fruit or vegetable, so be sure to buy organic.

INGREDIENTS

24 ounce filtered water

3 mint tea bags, ½ cup fresh mint leaves, or 1 tablespoon dried mint

ADD-INS

½ cup hulled, halved strawberries

Infused ice cubes (page 171; optional)

1 sprig mint for serving

METHOD

Place the water and tea bags or loose leaves in a lidded mason jar, cover, and refrigerate overnight. Remove the bags or strain out the leaves.

TO FURTHER INFUSE: Add strawberries to the jar, or a few fresh strawberries to a glass with some infused ice cubes and a sprig of mint to garnish.

PU-ERH COLD BREW INFUSION + ORANGE

Pu-erh's earthy taste is loved and revered by tea aficionados around the world. Pu-erh (pronounced "poo-air") is aged, fermented, and oxidized, which gives these leaves a chemical composition that produces amazing medicinal properties. Since it is considered a slimming tea, it has grown widely popular. Some people love the taste, and others not so much, but if you add a pinch of oolong or black tea along with the pu-erh, it makes a tastier drink for some palates. Try this infusion for more vitamins and a softer taste. Don't give up on flavoring this tea to please your taste buds, as it's worth all the health benefits and is a great morning coffee replacer. Purchase a good quality pu-erh online or at your tea dealer.

INGREDIENTS

24 ounces filtered water

2 pu-erh tea bags, or 1 tablespoon loose tea

1 orange tea bag, or ½ tablespoon dried orange peel (see page 168)

ADD-INS

2 fresh orange slices, peeled and seeded

Infused ice cubes (page 171; optional)

METHOD

Place the water, tea bags or loose tea, and dried orange peel (if using) in a lidded mason jar, cover, and refrigerate for 4 to 6 hours or overnight. Remove the bags or strain out the loose tea (and orange peel, if necessary).

TO FURTHER INFUSE: Place fresh orange slices in jar and sip this tea throughout the day. Infused ice cubes may be added to each serving.

PU-ERH

In an article on Healthline's website, Debra Rose Wilson, PhD, claims pu-erh has many potential health benefits. Pu-erh is antibacterial, anti-inflammatory, antiaging, and can help break down and release body toxins. Pu-erh may aid digestion as well. The gamma aminobutyric acid (GABA) found in pu-erh has been shown to reduce anxiety levels.

Chinese medicine credits pu-erh with the promotion of weight loss and with cardiovascular protection. Pu-erh may help improve sleep quality, lower blood sugar, and boost immunity. It may help promote bone health and lower the risk of osteoporosis. Research suggests that consuming five to eight cups a day can reduce cholesterol and plaque in the arteries. More research is being done on the effects of pu-erh and cancer, as pu-erh tea has been shown to inhibit the growth of tumor cells.

PASSION FRUIT COLD BREW INFUSION + ORANGE

Several companies carry passion fruit leaves for use in infusions, but make sure what you purchase is high quality and not just flavored, synthetic, or mixed with black tea. Loose leaves over bags may be the best way to ensure quality. Every brand is different, so know your supplier.

INGREDIENTS

24 ounces filtered water

3 passion fruit tea bags, or 2 tablespoons loose leaves

ADD-INS

2 orange slices or a squeeze of orange juice

METHOD

Place the water and tea bags or loose leaves in a lidded mason jar, cover, and refrigerate for 6 hours or overnight. Remove the bags or strain out the loose leaves.

TO FURTHER INFUSE: Add the orange slices or a squeeze of orange juice.

PASSION FRUIT

Since ancient times, passion fruit has been cultivated because of its influence on the immune system. Pure passion fruit leaves are said to be helpful for sleep problems, digestive issues, anxiety, and nervousness, and could act as a muscle relaxer. Although more evidence is needed, passion fruit may help to lower high blood pressure and aid in heart problems, fibromyalgia, asthma, and other health conditions.

ROSE HIPS COLD BREW INFUSION + STRAWBERRY, ORANGE, OR APPLE

A rose hip infusion is a great detoxifier and claims many benefits, including being good for skin, reducing inflammation, and strengthening immunity. Rose hips infusions contain vitamin C, flavonoids, polyphenols, other phytochemicals, and are rich in iron. Native Americans have used this tea for hundreds of years to fight off colds and flu. Many people drink rose hips not for the health benefits but for its tasty goodness, which is slightly tart, like cranberries. I love the tartness, but by adding a sweet fruit infusion, rose hips can transform into a delightful brew.

INGREDIENTS

24 ounces filtered water

3 rose hips tea bags, or 1½ tablespoons loose rose hips

ADD-INS

½ cup chopped strawberries, orange, or apple

Infused ice cubes (see page 171)

METHOD

Place the water and tea bags or loose rose hips in a lidded mason jar, cover, and refrigerate for 6 hours or overnight. Remove the bags or strain out the rose hips.

TO FURTHER INFUSE: Add strawberries, orange, or apple, or all three fruits. Serve in a glass with infused ice cubes.

YERBA MATÉ COLD BREW INFUSION + DRIED ORANGE + MINT

Yerba maté is indigenous to South America and traditionally steeped hot in a maté gourd and consumed through a metal straw called a *bombilla*. It is known for energizing and rejuvenating. It is believed to enhance endurance, support clarity, and produce a feeling of well-being. The caffeine content is still being debated, but drinkers of this tea attest to its health attributes. It is a good coffee replacer and afternoon pick-me-up. Depending on how long it is steeped, this can be a strong-tasting drink. Infusing with orange or mint adds to the flavor, but once you get hooked on the taste, you just might be drinking it straight. The quality of the maté you purchase really makes a difference.

INGREDIENTS

24 ounces filtered water

3 yerba maté tea bags, or 1 tablespoon loose tea

ADD-INS

2 orange slices, rind removed

1 sprig mint

Infused ice cubes (see page 171)

METHOD

Place the water and the tea bags or loose tea in a lidded jar, cover, and refrigerate overnight. In the morning, remove the bags or strain out the loose tea.

TO FURTHER INFUSE: Add orange slices and mint. Pour into a pretty glass and add infused ice cubes and you will have an exciting drink.

YERBA MATÉ

Yerba maté is loaded with vitamins A, C, B-complex, and E, and it contains magnesium, manganese, calcium, potassium, iron, and zinc. It makes a really tasty iced latte as well as a hot drink. For a cold latte, place the infusion in a blender, add ¼ cup of nondairy milk (coconut or almond are yummy), a bit of sweetener, and ice cubes, and blitz until well combined, or mix together by hand.

HOT HERBAL INFUSIONS

A warm cup of tea can be very relaxing, soothing, and comforting. I remember giving my children a cup of warm tea if they were under the weather. They always felt better after drinking the tea, and so did I.

ALFALFA HOT WATER INFUSION + RASPBERRIES

Alfalfa infusion is made only with the seeds and dried leaves of the plant. Drink this infusion for strength and well-being. The taste is very earthy and the aroma can be relaxing. You can purchase alfalfa for infusions in tea bags or loose from a reputable organic tea company.

INGREDIENTS

8 ounces filtered water

1 heaping teaspoon crushed alfalfa seeds, or 1 alfalfa tea bag

¼ cup fresh raspberries, or ½ teaspoon dried raspberry leaves

METHOD

Place the water and alfalfa seeds or tea bag, plus raspberry leaves, if using, in a pot over medium heat and simmer for 5 minutes. Turn off the heat, cover, and steep for 10 to 12 minutes. Strain out the seeds (and leaves) or discard the bag.

If using fresh raspberries, place them in a cup and pour the infusion over them.

ALFALFA

Alfalfa is commonly known as fodder for cows, but it's medicinal as well. It is rich in nutrients and minerals and useful for fighting heart disease. Additionally, it is an anti-inflammatory for the bladder and rheumatism. Alfalfa infusion relieves bloating and constipation, as it works as a diuretic.

BORAGE HOT WATER INFUSION + SLICED ORANGE

If you have a garden, borage is a great companion plant and is easy to grow.

INGREDIENTS

8 ounces filtered water

1 to 3 tablespoons fresh borage, or 1 to 3 teaspoons dried borage

2 orange slices

METHOD

Lightly boil the water in a lidded pot. Turn off the heat and add the borage. Cover and steep for 10 to 15 minutes. Strain out the leaves. Place the orange slices in a cup and pour the infusion over them. Lightly sweeten, if desired.

BORAGE

Borage infusion is a restorative for the adrenal glands, which help the body release stress, anxiety, depression, and nervous tension. It cleans the blood, releases fever, and helps detoxify and release poisons. Borage is used to relieve colds and coughs.

CALENDULA HOT WATER INFUSION + STRAWBERRIES

Aside from their medicinal qualities, calendula flowers have a pleasant aroma and are beautiful to look at.

INGREDIENTS

8 ounces filtered water

2 teaspoons calendula flowers, or 1 calendula tea bag

ADD-INS

2 hulled and sliced strawberries

METHOD

Lightly boil the water in a lidded pot. Turn off the heat and add the calendula flowers or tea bag. Steep, covered, for 15 minutes. Strain out the flowers or remove the bag.

TO FURTHER INFUSE: Add sliced strawberries.

CALENDULA

Calendula is known to be used for urinary tract infections and skin irritations, and to promote healing. It is anti-inflammatory and antiviral, calms muscle spasms, soothes the throat, improves oral health, aids digestion, calms the GI tract, and may help prevent macular degeneration.

CHAMOMILE HOT WATER INFUSION + LEMON

Chamomile is a soothing herb. By adding lemon to your herb infusion, you get an alkalizing effect as well.

INGREDIENTS

8 ounces filtered water

1 chamomile tea bag or 1 to 2 teaspoons loose tea

½ lemon, thinly sliced, plus more to serve (optional)

METHOD

Lightly boil the water in a lidded pot. Turn off the heat, add the tea bags or loose tea and lemon, and steep 6 for 8 minutes. Remove the bag or strain out the blossoms and the lemon slices and pour into a cup. Add fresh lemon slices, if desired, to garnish. If you want to sip this tea warm throughout the day, double or triple the recipe and use a carafe to keep it warm.

CHAMOMILE

Chamomile may help fight anxiety and depression. It is anti-inflammatory and a natural remedy for menstrual disorders. It is also good for insomnia.

BURDOCK ROOT HOT WATER INFUSION + PINEAPPLE OR POMEGRANATE JUICE

You can purchase fresh burdock root or tea bags from a tea dealer or Asian market. Choose a firm root. The color can be dark or light. Although the lighter color makes a nice infusion, it does not keep as well. Clean the root by scraping the skin with the edge of a knife. Chopped burdock root may be dehydrated and brewed dried.

CAUTION: Because burdock is a diuretic, if you are on medications, check with your health-care professional before using.

INGREDIENTS

8 ounces filtered water

2 tablespoons chopped burdock root

2 tablespoons unsweetened pineapple or pomegranate juice

METHOD

Place the water and burdock in a stainless steel pot and simmer for 15 to 20 minutes. Turn off the heat, cover, and steep for 10 minutes. Strain out the root, add the pineapple or pomegranate juice, and stir together. Pour into a cup to serve. If you would like to sip this infusion throughout the day, double or triple the recipe and keep it warm in a thermos.

BURDOCK ROOT

Burdock root tea is an effective remedy for eczema, acne, and psoriasis, and rids the body of excess water weight. It soothes arthritis and rheumatism. Folk medicine claims burdock helps with hair loss, is a blood purifier, and aids regeneration of liver cells.

DANDELION HOT WATER INFUSION + DRIED ORANGE PEEL

To most people with lawns, dandelions are their arch nemeses. Dandelions are considered a weed and homeowners want to get rid of them. They pull them out of the ground, poison them, and find them a nuisance. If they only knew the benefits of this plant, they might give it a little more respect. The stem or little yellow floret can be eaten raw, boiled, or made into herbal infusions. To be sure the dandelions have not been sprayed with pesticides or herbicides, don't just pick them from someone's lawn; grow them organically yourself, buy fresh organic dandelion from a natural foods store, or purchase loose tea or tea bags.

INGREDIENTS

2 teaspoons fresh dandelion flowers and stems, 1 tablespoon dried, or 1 dandelion tea bag

8 ounces filtered water

1 teaspoon dried orange peel (see page 168)

METHOD

If using fresh, wash the dandelion flowers and stems in a strainer under running water. Place the filtered water in a pot and add the fresh or dried dandelion. Simmer over medium-low heat for 10 to 12 minutes. Turn off the heat, cover, and steep for 3 minutes, then strain and pour into a cup. If using a tea bag, lightly boil the water, place the tea bag in a cup, and pour the water over it. Cover with a saucer and let steep for 4 to 6 minutes. Add the orange peel to the cup for extra flavor and vitamin C.

DANDELION GREENS

Dandelion greens contain antioxidants, potassium, dietary fiber, and vitamins A, B_6, C, and K; they also contain calcium, iron, and magnesium. Dandelion is used for the treatment of muscle aches, upset stomach, gallstones, and bruises, and for rejuvenation. It cleanses the liver, aids the digestive system, reduces inflammation, fights diabetes, and treats viral infections. By drinking dandelion infusion or eating the flowers and green parts, you may avoid bone loss, tooth decay, muscle tension, high blood pressure, and calcium deficiency.

ECHINACEA HOT WATER INFUSION + MINT + LEMON

Echinacea is a flowering perennial plant in the daisy family. Different parts of the echinacea plant, including its flowers, leaves, stem, and root, contain a variety of phenolic compounds that are beneficial to health. Native Americans have used echinacea for hundreds of years in their herbal remedies to boost immunity and fight infections. Echinacea should not be overused; a cup or two a day when feeling a cold or sore throat coming on is fine, and when you need it, nothing works better. The spearmint and lemon add to its flavor and healing properties.

INGREDIENTS

8 ounces filtered water

**1 echinacea tea bag, or 2 teaspoons dried loose tea or
a small handful of fresh leaves and stems**

2 sprigs spearmint

1 lemon slice

METHOD

Lightly boil the water. Place the tea bag or loose tea, mint, and lemon slice in a cup and pour the water over them. Cover with a saucer and steep for 5 to 7 minutes. Strain and add the spearmint and lemon slice.

ECHINACEA

Echinacea has been known to boost the immune system and help prevent colds, as well as to assist with respiratory issues. Echinacea eliminates bacterial and viral infections, reduces inflammation, regulates blood sugar levels, and eases anxiety.

EYEBRIGHT HOT WATER INFUSION + LEMON

Eyebright leaves for an herbal infusion can be purchased online. Choose wild organic or at least organic leaves.

INGREDIENTS

8 ounces filtered water

1 eyebright tea bag, 2 tablespoons loose fresh leaves, or 1 teaspoon dried eyebright

1 or 2 lemon slices for serving

Sweetener (see page 26; optional)

METHOD

Lightly boil the water. Place the tea bag or loose tea in a cup and pour in the water. Cover with a saucer and let steep for 5 to 7 minutes. Remove the bag or strain out the leaves.

To serve, place the lemon slices in the cup and sweeten, if desired.

EYEBRIGHT

The name says it all. Eyebright is helpful for eye strain, inflammation of the eye, and other eye ailments, including itchy or dry eyes. Drinking eyebright tea may improve memory, as it is high in beta-carotenes. The antibacterial properties of this tea make it a good topical healer as well. Eyebright infusion can be used topically on the eye by placing a clean cotton pad or cloth into the room temperature tea and placing on the closed eyelid. It is safe if the tea enters the eye and will soothe tired eyes after looking at a computer all day. Be sure that everything you use is sterilized and the tea is organic if you are using it topically on your eyes.

GINGER HOT WATER INFUSION + LEMON

No tea bag necessary or desired. Use fresh ginger for the best-tasting infusion with tons of medicinal properties. Feel free to mix and match the fruit or use more fruit if you like.

INGREDIENTS

16 ounces filtered water

**One 2-inch piece fresh ginger, thinly sliced
(if organic, no need to scrape off the skin)**

2 lemon slices, or ½ cup fresh mint, raspberries, or dried apricots

METHOD

Place the water and ginger in a lidded pot and simmer over medium-low heat for 5 minutes. Turn off the heat, cover, and steep for 4 to 6 minutes. Let the water cool down for a few minutes, then pour into a heatproof lidded container or glass jar. Add the fruit and marinate, covered, for 10 to 20 minutes. The ginger can be removed when the taste is to your liking, anywhere from 15 minutes to 2 hours. Serve warm or refrigerate for iced tea. If serving cold, add infused ice cubes.

GINGER

Ginger infusion is a great drink if you suffer from motion sickness or nausea. It is good for digestion and increasing the absorption of food, relieves bloating, and is anti-inflammatory, which makes it ideal for muscle and joint pains. Ginger helps relieve respiratory problems that accompany a cold and congestion, and may help increase blood circulation, which can aid with cardiovascular problems. Ginger decreases blood sugar levels, lowers cholesterol, helps with menstrual cramps, combats infections, aids osteoarthritis, and sharpens brain function. Ginger tea can relieve stress and boost your immune system. Ginger contains a compound called 6-gingerol, and early studies show promise that this compound might slow or stop cancer cell growth in prostate, pancreatic, and ovarian cancers. However, no scientific conclusion has been made as of yet.

GINGER HOT WATER INFUSION + PEAR + LIME

This immunity-boosting infusion is very invigorating to start your morning. Adding pear and lime boosts its antioxidants and vitamins.

INGREDIENTS

8 ounces filtered water

**One 2-inch piece fresh ginger, thinly sliced
(if organic, no need to scrape off the skin)**

½ small pear, cored and thinly sliced

1 teaspoon fresh lime juice

Sweetener (see page 26; optional)

METHOD

Place the water and ginger in a lidded pot and simmer over medium-low heat for 5 minutes. Add the pear slices, cover, and steep for 4 to 5 minutes. Taste to decide whether the tea is to your liking; if not, cover again and steep for 5 to 8 minutes longer. Feel free to use more ginger if you enjoy the flavor. Pour into a cup and add the lime juice and sweetener to taste, if desired.

GOLDENROD HOT WATER INFUSION + CITRUS

The name goldenrod covers about 100 to 120 different species of flowering plants from the Aster family. These yellow flowers grow wild in meadows and prairies.

INGREDIENTS

8 ounces filtered water

2 tablespoons fresh goldenrod flowers, or 1 tablespoon dried goldenrod

ADD-INS

2 slices of citrus fruit of choice

METHOD

Lightly boil the water. Place the flowers in a cup and pour the water over them. Cover with a saucer and steep for 15 to 20 minutes. Strain out the flowers.

TO FURTHER INFUSE: Add sliced citrus of your choice.

GOLDENROD

Use goldenrod infusion to help relieve symptoms of bladder infection, kidney stones, or urinary tract infections. Goldenrod helps relieve cold and flu symptoms and is good for the respiratory tract. Goldenrod is said to help with colic, diarrhea, and stomach cramps. Drink this infusion for allergies, diabetes, asthma, dental infections, and fungal infections.

GOTU KOLA HOT WATER INFUSION + MANGO

Popular in parts of Asia, gotu kola leaves, from the flowering *Centella asiatica* plant, are used to make a subtle and soothing light infusion. Succulent mango is a high-antioxidant fruit, which aids in supporting many health issues. Mango can lower cholesterol, clear the skin, improve eye health, and alkalize the body, just to name a few of its benefits. Be sure to eat the mango after infusing the water.

INGREDIENTS

8 ounces filtered water

1 tablespoon gotu kola leaves, or 1 gotu kola tea bag

1 to 2 tablespoons chopped mango

Fresh mint leaves (optional)

METHOD

Lightly boil the water. Place the leaves or tea bag in a cup and pour in the water. Add the mango, cover the cup with a saucer, and steep for 6 to 8 minutes. Strain out the leaves or remove the bag. Add mint leaves, if desired.

GOTU KOLA

Gotu kola is known for improving mental focus and relieving tension and anxiety. It improves digestive health, eliminates congestion, improves circulation, and relieves pain and swelling.

VALERIAN ROOT HOT WATER INFUSION + ORANGE SQUEEZE

It is best not to drink this tea during the day unless you want to fall asleep at your desk. Valerian root is the sleepy tea you always wanted. Valerian root will put most people to sleep. It's natural, so no worries about being addicted to sleeping pills. In fact, stay away from sleep aids. With valerian, most people won't need anything else, as it's considered a mild sedative. Who doesn't want a good night's sleep after a long day at work?

INGREDIENTS

8 ounces filtered water

1 valerian root tea bag, or 2 teaspoons loose valerian root

Squeeze of orange juice (optional)

METHOD

Lightly boil the water. Place the tea bag or loose leaves in a cup and pour in the water. Cover with a saucer and steep for 4 to 5 minutes. Remove the bag or strain out the leaves and drink before bedtime. No other infusion is necessary, but if you'd like it sweeter, add a squeeze of orange juice.

VALERIAN

Valerian relieves muscle pain, anxiety, headaches, and even menopausal hot flashes.

GINKGO BILOBA HOT WATER INFUSION + BERRIES OR ORANGE

This tea is naturally caffeine-free and could replace coffee, as its brain-boosting components provide mental clarity. *Ginkgo biloba* is also known as maidenhair and is a tree originally from China. Studies show that the tree existed 200 million years ago. The leaves, fruits, seeds, and bark can be used to improve a variety of ailments; indeed, ginkgo is used as a prescription herb in Germany. The tea, made from the leaves, is considered an herbal infusion.

CAUTION: If you take anticoagulants or antithrombotic medicine, if you are pregnant or breastfeeding, or have had seizures, check with your doctor before drinking ginkgo tea.

INGREDIENTS

8 ounces filtered water

2 tablespoons ginkgo leaves, or 1 ginkgo tea bag

¼ cup sweet berries or orange slices

METHOD

Boil the water just until medium-size bubbles start to appear. Turn off the heat, place the leaves or tea bag in the water, cover, and steep for 6 to 8 minutes. Strain out the leaves or remove the bag. Place the fruit in the bottom of a cup and pour the infusion over the fruit. While drinking, think of all the positive benefits of this healing tea.

GINKGO BILOBA

Ginkgo biloba tea contains a high amount of antioxidants. It helps promote longevity and increases concentration. This infusion can help stimulate blood circulation and it's said that, if consumed daily, this tea can relieve Raynaud's disease, which is caused by restricted blood flow in the fingers and toes. Its ability to reduce blood viscosity and to increase vascular dilation may help reduce retina damage due to macular degeneration and may reverse deafness caused by reduced blood flow. Ginkgo tea also minimizes blood coagulation, cramps, and headaches and reduces clogging of arteries by inhibiting plaque formation, making this a heart-healthy drink. Drinking this infusion can remove toxins and help lower cholesterol, and create a sense of well-being. *Ginkgo biloba* can help with hormonal imbalance and mood swings.

PARSLEY HOT WATER INFUSION +
DRIED OR FRESH LEMON

This light-tasting infusion is quite delicious and a different taste than when you eat parsley.

INGREDIENTS

8 ounces filtered water

6 sprigs fresh parsley, 1 tablespoon dried parsley leaves, or 1 parsley tea bag

Generous pinch of dried lemon zest, or 1 fresh slice (optional)

METHOD

Lightly boil the water in a lidded pot. Turn off heat, add the sprigs or leaves or tea bag, cover, and steep for 8 to 10 minutes. If you don't mind the leaves, they can be left in your cup while you drink the infusion. Parsley tea is best tasting without any additional ingredients, but a little lemon zest or fresh lemon can be added, if desired.

PARSLEY

Parsley relieves anemia, indigestion, gout, and bad breath, and is used as a diuretic, which can promote weight loss. It is also known for antiaging, kidney cleansing, rheumatism, and arthritis. Parsley contains vitamin A, B-complex, and C, and as it is high in iron, it might mitigate with bone loss.

PEPPERMINT HOT WATER INFUSION + PINEAPPLE OR ORANGE

Peppermint is strong and infuses quickly, so taste after steeping for a few minutes to see when it's right for you.

INGREDIENTS

8 ounces filtered water

1 peppermint tea bag, or 1 teaspoon loose peppermint leaves

½ cup pineapple chunks, or 2 orange slices

METHOD

Boil the water in a lidded pot just until medium-size bubbles start to appear. Turn off the heat, add the tea bag or loose leaves, cover, and steep for 3 to 4 minutes. Place the fruit in the bottom of the cup and pour the infusion over the fruit. Inhale the fragrance and enjoy.

PEPPERMINT

Peppermint is known for many health benefits, including improving digestion. It reduces fever, boosts immunity, stops nausea, helps with weight loss, calms stress, improves breath, and soothes irritable bowel syndrome.

ROSEBUD OR ROSE PETAL HOT WATER INFUSION + LEMON VERBENA

Rose buds and petals can be purchased dried from herbal tea stores or online. Always purchase organic. If you grow your own roses pesticide-free, you can make your own dried buds or rose petals by drying them in the sun or in a dehydrator. The sweet aroma of rose infusion may bring about a romantic feeling. I recommend sitting outside on the terrace or patio and sipping a cup or two while practicing self-love.

INGREDIENTS

12 ounces filtered water

2 tablespoons dried rosebuds or petals

1 teaspoon dried lemon verbena

Sweetener (see page 26; optional)

METHOD

Lightly boil the water in a lidded pot. Turn off the heat, place the rosebuds or rose petals and lemon verbena in a generously sized infuser and place in the pot, or place them directly in the pot and stir to be sure all buds or petals are absorbing the water. Cover and steep for 7 to 10 minutes. Strain out the buds or petals and pour the infusion into a cup or small bowl you can hold in the palm of your hands. Add sweetener, if desired.

ROSES

Rosebud tea is packed with vitamins A, E, and especially C—surpassing the vitamin C in orange, tomato, and grapefruit. Rose tea works as a diuretic and helps with weight loss. Roses have antiseptic prosperities; they are antibacterial, antioxidative, and anti-inflammatory. Drinking a rose infusion is said to be good for improving digestion and blood circulation and helps build a strong immune system. Applied topically, rose infusion nourishes the skin and makes a good facial wash.

ROSEMARY HOT WATER INFUSION + STRAWBERRIES

Rosemary is an herb that has been used for centuries for its medicinal benefits.

CAUTION: If you are pregnant or breastfeeding, always check with your health-care professional before consuming rosemary tea.

INGREDIENTS

8 ounces filtered water

1 or 2 sprigs fresh rosemary, or 1½ teaspoons loose leaves, or 1 rosemary tea bag

2 strawberries, hulled and cut in half

Sweetener (see page 26; optional)

METHOD

Lightly boil the water in a lidded pot. Shut off the heat, add the rosemary sprigs or leaves, cover, and steep for 6 to 10 minutes. Alternatively, for a stronger infusion, place the rosemary in the unboiled water and lightly simmer for 5 minutes, shut off the heat, cover, and steep for 4 minutes. Strain out the leaves or remove the bag. Place the strawberries in a cup and pour the infusion on top. Add sweetener, if desired.

ROSEMARY

Drinking rosemary tea is good for Alzheimer's or other dementia, digestion, arthritis, anxiety, hair loss, high blood pressure, chronic pain, detoxifying the liver, skin conditions, inflammation, and depression.

SAGE HOT WATER INFUSION + BLACKBERRY

Blackberries are best when they are in season, both for taste and price, and they can easily be frozen to enjoy at a later time.

INGREDIENTS

8 ounces filtered water

2 tablespoons fresh sage leaves, or 1 tablespoon dried, or 1 sage tea bag

¼ cup blackberries

METHOD

Place the water and sage leaves or tea bag in a lidded pot and lightly simmer over medium-low heat for 5 minutes. Shut off the heat, cover, and steep for 8 to 10 minutes. Strain out the leaves or remove the bag. Place the blackberries in a cup and pour the infusion over them. Crush the blackberries with a spoon to release their sweetness. Be sure to eat the blackberries after you finish your drink to receive all their benefits.

SAGE

Throughout the centuries, sage infusions have been used for brain stimulation and clear thinking. Sage might have memory-boosting properties and helps with Alzheimer's and other dementia. It is said to balance cholesterol and help with weight loss. The essential oils are good for the skin and sage has antiaging benefits because of its high antioxidant component. A sage infusion is anti-inflammatory, treats indigestion, relieves a sore throat, and is good for dental health. It may help diabetes and asthma, and has neurological benefits.

SPEARMINT HOT WATER INFUSION + LAVENDER

Spearmint tea is best when the leaves are used fresh. If not available, loose dried tea or tea bags will do, but once you taste the fresh mint in your water, you will long to grow some in your garden so it's always available. Mint is easy to grow in pots, so give it a try. If you love green tea as I do, you can always use a green tea bag or some loose tea along with the fresh mint. A pinch of lavender calms the nerves and aids depression and digestion.

INGREDIENTS

8 ounces filtered water

4 sprigs fresh spearmint, 1 tablespoon loose leaves, or 2 spearmint tea bags

A generous pinch of culinary lavender buds

METHOD

Boil the water just until medium-size bubbles start to appear. Place the fresh mint and lavender in a heatproof glass. Allow the water to cool slightly, put a spoon in the glass, and slowly pour the water over the spoon. Let 1 or 2 inches of water warm the glass before filling with the balance of hot water. The spoon helps conduct away some of the heat to prevent the glass from breaking. Let steep for 8 to 10 minutes. Mint leaves do not have to be removed while drinking, but strain out the lavender. Alternatively, if using a spearmint tea bag, lightly boil the water in a lidded pot, turn off the heat, add the tea bag and lavender, cover, and steep for 3 to 4 minutes. Remove the bag and strain out the buds.

SPEARMINT

Besides the wonderful flavor, spearmint is good for many things, including boosting the immune system, eliminating nausea, improving memory, balancing hormone levels, reducing inflammation, and preventing fungal infections.

STINGING NETTLE HOT WATER INFUSION +
MINT + LEMON

Nettles come up in spring. They grow wild and look innocent. They are common weeds throughout the world and can be found in partial shade along a fence or at the edge of the forest. The leaves are heart-shaped with sawlike edges, and grow in pairs. Pick in spring before the plant flowers. Stinging nettles are covered with small spines or stickers. You can't see them, but you will certainly feel them if you brush up against the leaves or try to pick them without gloves. These stickers deliver histamines into the skin of humans and animals alike. Be sure to wear rubber or heavy garden gloves, long sleeves, and long pants to avoid the little stickers. Use scissors or garden clippers to clip them into a bag. The stems can also be used for tea. Wash fresh leaves in a strainer under running water. If you soak them in water, the stickers neutralize, making the plant harmless. The leaves can be used fresh or dried. To dry, just leave them in the bag in a well-ventilated room until dried, or dry in the sun.

Stinging nettle infusion can be found dried and in tea bags, but fresh leaves can be boiled directly into water to make an infusion.

CAUTION: Because this tea lowers blood sugar levels, avoid if you are diabetic or hypoglycemic or take blood pressure medication or other medications. Avoid nettle tea if you are pregnant or breastfeeding. Consult with your health-care professional before consuming nettle infusions.

INGREDIENTS

1 cup fresh nettle leaves, or 1 tablespoon dried nettle leaves

16 ounces filtered water

1 lemon slice

2 sprigs mint

METHOD

Lightly simmer the nettle leaves in the water for 10 minutes, or until the water turns green, then strain and transfer the infusion to a cup. Alternatively put the leaves in a cup and pour hot water over them. Cover with a saucer and let steep until the water turns green, then strain out the leaves. If you like it stronger, just steep a little longer. To serve, add the lemon slice and mint to your cup. If you use a squeeze of lemon, the tea will turn pink and give the nettle a lovely taste.

NETTLE

Here is why nettle is worth seeking out. Nettle tea contains flavonoids, carotenoids, and vitamins A, B-complex, C, D, and K. Nettle leaves are comparable to leafy green vegetables, as they contain calcium and magnesium. In particular, the benefits of the leaves resemble those of spinach, as they are protein-dense and contain iodine, iron, potassium, and silicon. Stinging nettle stimulates hair growth, controls blood sugar, treats disorders of the kidney, is good for gums, and treats diarrhea. They are known to improve prostate health, skin rashes, and scarring of the skin. Stinging nettle protects heart health and may relieve osteoarthritis and gout. This tea can improve digestion, reduce inflammation, boost immunity, treat menstrual cramps, and help with weight loss.

THYME HOT WATER INFUSION + LEMON + CINNAMON BARK

The aroma of thyme infusion is known to lift your mood. Add a bit of cinnamon for an extra boost. Thyme is from the mint family; avoid if you are allergic to mint.

INGREDIENTS

8 ounces filtered water

1 teaspoon fresh thyme leaves, ½ teaspoon dried, or 1 thyme tea bag

1 lemon slice

One 1-inch piece cinnamon bark

Sweetener (optional)

METHOD

Combine the water and thyme leaves or bag, lemon, and cinnamon bark in a lidded pot and lightly simmer over medium-low heat for 5 to 7 minutes. Turn off the heat, cover the pot, and steep for 4 to 5 minutes. Strain out the leaves (or remove the bag), lemon, and cinnamon. Pour the infusion into a cup, add sweetener, if desired, and enjoy.

THYME

Most people think of thyme as a culinary herb, but thyme hot water infusion is full of medicinal benefits and a good way to reap the rewards of this herb. Thyme is antimicrobial, is said to lower blood pressure and cholesterol, and relieves a cough or sore throat. Thyme infusion soothes digestion, aids sleep, boosts the immune system, and relieves menstrual cramps. The herb is packed with vitamins A and C.

TULSI HOT WATER INFUSION + GINGER + MINT

Tulsi, also called holy basil or Thai basil, is an herb used in Ayurvedic medicine. It has a slightly minty clove taste.

INGREDIENTS

8 ounces filtered water

1 small handful fresh tulsi leaves, washed, or 1 tablespoon dried tulsi leaves, or 1 tulsi tea bag

2 thin slices fresh ginger (optional)

1 sprig fresh mint

METHOD

Place the water and the leaves or tea bag in a lidded pot and lightly simmer over medium-low heat for 6 minutes. Shut off the heat and add the ginger, if using, and mint. Cover the pot and infuse for 3 to 4 minutes. Drink hot, or refrigerate to serve as iced tea.

TULSI (HOLY BASIL OR THAI BASIL)

Tulsi is rich in antioxidants, which helps the body fight free radicals that are responsible for causing degenerative diseases. It is known to boost the immune system, strengthen the heart, and improve memory; relieve asthma, bronchitis, headache, stomach upset, fever, and viral infection; and reduce stress; and may help promote healthy vision and oral health.

COLD BREW FRUIT INFUSIONS

I am so excited for you to try homemade cold brew infusions. They are so easy to make, and you don't even have to boil water! When you cold brew tea and herbs, all the health benefits and flavor from the leaves or bag are extracted. The brew is never bitter because of the slow extraction method. Let the hydration party begin.

LEMON COLD BREW INFUSION + BASIL

By now, you know the benefits of lemon, especially if you've made a cold brew lemon infusion. Basil is a popular herb for cooking but, when infused in lemon water, it is a great way to get some quick health benefits as well as great taste. This simple and quick-to-prepare tea is good for the digestive tract and the potassium in basil and lemon may help counteract bloat. This tea contains antioxidants, which protect your body from pollutants.

INGREDIENTS

24 ounces filtered water

2 lemon tea bags, or 1 tablespoon loose lemon tea

3 or 4 fresh basil leaves

2 lemon slices, peeled and seeded

Infused ice cubes (see page 171)

METHOD

Place the water and tea bags or loose tea in a lidded mason jar, cover, and refrigerate for 6 hours, then add the basil and lemon slices. Place back in the refrigerator and infuse overnight, then remove the bags or strain out the leaves. The basil and lemon can stay longer, but if you like the taste the way it is, remove them. Pour into a glass with infused ice cubes for a refreshing drink.

BASIL

Basil is a wonderful cleanser, as it flushes out the body and is good for constipation. It is an anti-inflammatory herb that helps relieve rheumatoid arthritis; it also enhances circulation and stabilizes blood sugar.

LEMON COLD BREW INFUSION + BLACKBERRIES

Loose lemon leaves may be mixed with lemon verbena, which is always tasty. This flavor combination makes a thirst-quenching summer drink. As with all brews, drink at least 32 ounces a day for best results.

INGREDIENTS

24 ounces filtered water

2 tablespoons loose lemon tea, or 2 lemon tea bags

5 to 7 blackberries

2 lemon slices

METHOD

Place the water and loose tea or tea bags in a lidded mason jar and refrigerate for 6 hours or overnight. Strain out the tea or remove the bags. Add the blackberries and muddle them to release some of the juices. Squeeze the juice from the lemon slices into the infusion and place the lemon slices into the container as well. After 2 hours, remove rinds so as not to bitter the infusion.

LEMON + BLACKBERRIES

A good-quality lemon infusion with blackberries contains polyphenolic antioxidants, such as anthocyanin pigments, which are associated with optimal health. This infusion boosts the immune system, protects the heart, decreases inflammation, regulates hormones, prevents nausea and gastrointestinal issues, and helps with weight control.

PEACH COLD BREW INFUSION + CINNAMON STICK

There are many peach tea bags on the market, but most are made with blends and flavorings. Look for dried leaves of the peach tree from a reputable tea dealer. Cinnamon has been used medicinally for thousands of years and adding it to this infusion will boost its health benefits. Researchers say cinnamon is the number one spice in terms of protective antioxidant levels. For the best flavor and nutritional value, use cinnamon sticks or bark instead of powdered cinnamon.

INGREDIENTS

24 ounces filtered water

2 tablespoons loose peach tea, or 2 high-quality peach tea bags;
alternatively, use a light tea, such as jasmine, white, or green, as a base

½ cup fresh, frozen, or dehydrated peaches (see sidebar)

1 cinnamon stick or a 2-inch piece of cinnamon bark

Mint-infused ice cubes (see page 171; optional)

METHOD

Place the water, loose tea or tea bags, and peaches in a lidded mason jar, cover, and refrigerate for 6 hours or overnight. Strain out the leaves or remove the bags. Add more peaches if you like, and sip throughout the day, eating the infused peaches as well. This drink is lovely served in a glass with infused peach, cinnamon stick or bark, and mint-infused ice cubes.

PEACHES

Peaches are loaded with minerals (including calcium, potassium, magnesium, iron, zinc, phosphorus, and manganese) and are rich in antioxidants, which are good for eye health. They aid digestion, soothe the nervous system, and are antiaging. The compounds in peaches may help lower cholesterol levels, boost immunity, and detoxify the body.

The Perfect Peach

Peaches today do not taste like the peaches I remember from my younger years. Today, you wait for peaches to ripen, only to find them tasteless and mushy. The best way to purchase peaches is when they are in season, preferably at your farmers' market. Most vendors have samples so you can taste before you purchase. Peaches, like any thin-skinned fruit, should always be purchased organic. When you find the sweetest and juiciest ones, buy as many as you can fit into your shopping basket. Peaches bruise easily, so be gentle with them. When you arrive home, set them out single file on the kitchen counter or a table to ripen to the touch. You want them not too hard, but not too soft, either. When they feel ripe, which could be in two to three days, eat as many as you can before they get too ripe.

Here is how to preserve your peach bounty, so when you get the craving for a peach-infused brew, they are always ready, during any season.

- Peel and pit some of the peaches and puree in a food processor or blender. Add a little water, if necessary, to make it pourable. Pour the peach liquid into ice cube trays and freeze. When frozen, transfer the cubes to resealable plastic freezer bags to store. Frozen peach ice cubes may be used in cold brew infusions or in smoothies.

- To freeze sliced peaches, first blanch the peaches for a second or two in boiling water, just long enough to make it easy to remove the skins. Immediately place the blanched peaches in an ice bath, so they don't continue to heat. The skins should be easy to remove at this time. Slice and freeze in a single layer, not touching one another, on a parchment-lined baking sheet, then transfer to a resealable plastic freezer bag.

- Another way to preserve ripe peaches is to dehydrate them. Follow the manufacturer's directions for drying fruit in your dehydrator.

PEACH COLD BREW INFUSION + MINT + LEMON

You can make homemade peach tea in just a few minutes, without using peach tea leaves.

INGREDIENTS

24 ounces filtered water

3 white or jasmine tea bags, or 2 tablespoons loose tea

1 fresh or frozen peach, halved and pitted

ADD-INS

3 sprigs mint

2 teaspoons fresh lemon juice

Infused ice cubes (see page 171)

METHOD

Place the water and tea bags or loose tea in a lidded mason jar, cover, and refrigerate for 6 or more hours. Remove the bags or strain out the loose tea. Transfer 8 ounces of the infusion to a blender and add the peach, then blend together until smooth. Pour the liquid through a nut milk bag or a mesh strainer and add back to the original jar.

TO FURTHER INFUSE: Add the mint and lemon juice. Pour over infused ice cubes and garnish each serving with a mint sprig.

POMEGRANATE COLD BREW INFUSION + LEMON + LIME + MINT

All citrus contains vitamin C, and lemon helps alkalize the body. I frequently use lemon, lime, orange, and mint as the health benefits are vast. All good reasons to add citrus to a cold brew pomegranate infusion.

INGREDIENTS

24 ounces filtered water

3 pomegranate tea bags, or 1 tablespoon loose pomegranate tea

2 tablespoons fresh or store-bought unsweetened pomegranate juice (see sidebar)

½ lemon, sliced and seeded

½ lime, sliced and seeded

1 sprig mint

ADD-INS

Infused ice cubes (see page 171)

Simple maple syrup (see page 168; optional)

METHOD

Place the water and tea bags or loose tea in a lidded mason jar, cover, and refrigerate 6 hours or overnight. Remove the bags or strain out the loose tea. Add the pomegranate juice, citrus slices, and mint, and infuse for 3 to 4 hours (if you can wait that long). To serve, pour into a glass and add infused ice cubes for a refreshing drink. If desired, a dash of simple maple syrup may be added.

POMEGRANATE

Pomegranate is considered a superfood. It is high in antioxidants, boosts the immune system, lowers cholesterol, aids in preventing heart disease, helps tighten skin, and assists in controlling body fat.

Make Your Own Pomegranate Juice

To make your own fresh pomegranate juice, place the pomegranate in a bowl in the sink and fill with cold water to cover. Under water, cut the fruit in half and then into quarters. Continuing to hold the pomegranate under water, use your fingers to loosen the seeds. No need to discard the thin white membrane until all the seeds are in the bowl. However, you can discard the outer red skin as you go. When finished removing the seeds, the membrane will float to the top and you can slowly pour off the water and the membrane should separate itself and pour out. Any seeds stuck to the white part can be loosened at this time. When the membrane is gone, drain the seeds through a mesh strainer over a deep bowl. Roughly mash the seeds with a pestle or wooden spoon or the bottom of a glass to release their juices. Transfer the juice to a lidded container to use within the next few days. Freeze any leftover pomegranate juice in ice cube trays to add to other cold brew teas.

RASPBERRY COLD BREW INFUSION + DRIED LEMON PEEL

This combination provides a tart, sweet flavor. If you can find Meyer lemons, you will really enjoy their sweetness and floral smell. Try this infusion with both base options: one using lemon tea bags and the other using raspberry tea bags.

INGREDIENTS

24 ounces filtered water

3 lemon or raspberry tea bags, or 2 tablespoons lemon or raspberry loose tea

½ cup fresh or frozen raspberries

1 tablespoon dried lemon peel or lemon zest (see page 168)

Raspberry- or lemon-infused ice cubes (see page 171; optional)

1 sprig mint (optional)

METHOD

Place the water and your tea bags or loose tea of choice in a lidded mason jar, cover, and refrigerate for 6 hours or overnight. Remove the bags or strain out the loose tea. Add the raspberries and dried lemon and infuse for 4 hours or eat the raspberries as you sip the tea. This is a beautiful drink served in a wineglass with raspberry- or lemon-infused ice cubes. A sprig of mint is always a nice garnish.

LEMONS

Lemons, like oranges, contain vitamin C. Lemon is good for indigestion, fevers, detoxifying, and weight loss. If you need some blood pressure help, try lemon in your cold brew or hot infusions.

RASPBERRY COLD BREW INFUSION +
DRIED ORANGE PEEL

Traditional Medicinals makes beautiful flavors of organic teas and herbal infusions, including raspberry. Starting out with a fruit-flavor herbal tea bag and then infusing with fresh fruits or herbs makes any infusion stand out with its fresh, full-bodied flavor. Raspberry Leaf is a great base as its subtle but sweet flavor enhances herbal infusions. Once you feel comfortable experimenting your creativity will leave its mark on every drink.

INGREDIENTS

24 ounces filtered water

3 raspberry tea bags, or 2 tablespoons loose raspberry tea

½ cup fresh or frozen raspberries

**1 orange, peeled, sliced, and seeded, or 1 tablespoon
dried orange peel (see page 168)**

Raspberry- or orange-infused ice cubes (see page 171; optional)

1 sprig mint (optional)

METHOD

Place the water and tea in a lidded mason jar, cover, and refrigerate for 6 hours or overnight. Remove the bags or strain out the loose tea. Add the raspberries and orange and infuse for 4 hours, or eat the raspberries and oranges as you sip the infusion. This is lovely served in a wineglass with raspberry- or orange-infused ice cubes. A sprig of mint makes it even more tempting.

RASPBERRIES + ORANGES

Raspberries are high in antioxidants and contain ellagic acid, which is used to treat viral and bacterial infections. Raspberries are antiaging, good for weight loss, help prevent macular degeneration, and strengthen the immune system. Oranges are loaded with vitamin C and contain phytochemicals that can impact everything from hormones to your ability to fight off infections and diseases. These phytochemicals may help prevent kidney disease as well as lower cholesterol and risk of heart issues. For the full health benefits of this tea, eat the infused fruit.

FRUIT HOT WATER INFUSIONS

This is a simple, unique concept that will please your palate. All you need are your favorite fruits and filtered water. The flavors are subtle and light, but oh so delicious. These healthy infusions may just be the drink you need to warm your spirit.

DRIED APPLE HOT WATER INFUSION +
CINNAMON + LEMON

If you have a dehydrator, drying apples is one of the easiest things to do. If not, you can purchase one at your health food store or online.

INGREDIENTS

16 ounces filtered water

½ cup organic dried apples (no sugar or sulfur)

1 cinnamon stick

Juice of ½ lemon, rind reserved

METHOD

Place the water, dried apples, and a cinnamon stick in a pot. Simmer over medium-low heat for 10 to 15 minutes. Turn off the heat, cover, and let steep for another 10 minutes. Add the lemon juice and peel. Store in a thermos to drink throughout the day.

APPLES

Apples are very high in antioxidants, which helps neutralize free radicals. Free radicals cause oxidative stress, and increase your risk of chronic diseases. Apples benefit your immune system; are anti-inflammatory; and are good for heart health, vision, bone health, and fighting diabetes.

FRESH FRUIT HOT WATER TEA INFUSION + MINT + CHAMOMILE

Many years ago, on a trip to Bogotá, Colombia, I had one of the best teas I've ever tasted. This tea was full of nutrients because of all the fresh fruit it contained. It was my first hot fruit and herb infusion. It was served in a bowl, which intrigued me before I even tasted the luscious brew. It's been a staple for me since that day. Fresh mint is the base of this infusion. As you've already read, herbal mint infusions have many healing qualities; the fruit supplies nutrients as well as beneficial healing powers. This beautiful infusion might just be what you are looking for to serve guests or to have a bowl on your own.

INGREDIENTS

12 ounces filtered water

3 to 4 sprigs fresh mint

5 or 6 fresh or dried chamomile flowers or 1 chamomile tea bag

3 crisp apple slices

½ small guava or 2 segments mandarin orange

1 strawberry, hulled and cut in half

1 kiwi slice, peeled

3 or 4 dried hawthorn berries

ADD-INS

⅛ teaspoon culinary-grade lavender buds

Pinch of fresh thyme

1 small fresh sage leaf or pinch of dried sage

METHOD

Choose a bowl that is easy to hold with both hands so the aroma can be released and you can see the beauty of the fruits and herbs piled up in the bowl. Lightly boil the water and turn off the heat. Let cool for a couple of minutes. Place the mint, tea, and then the fruit in the bowl. For a dramatic effect, place the bowl in front of your guest, or yourself, and slowly pour the heated water into the bowl. This will release the aroma as the steam hits the mint and fruit. For a savory version, add lavender buds, thyme, and sage.

ORANGE PEEL HOT WATER INFUSION + STAR ANISE

Orange tea blended with star anise makes a delicious and healthy tea. This tea is a great after-dinner drink to help digestion and combat bloating and gas.

Loose dried orange pieces can be purchased, or you can easily make your own. Always buy organic when making orange or citrus peel tea, as sprayed citrus can contain up to six cancer-causing chemicals, twelve hormone-disrupting chemicals, and ten other disease-causing chemicals.

INGREDIENTS

8 ounces filtered water

1 tablespoon orange loose tea, or 1 orange tea bag

1 to 2 teaspoons dried orange peel (see page 168)

2 pieces dried star anise or a pinch of seeds

METHOD

Lightly boil the water in a lidded pot. Shut off the heat and place the loose tea or tea bag, orange peel, and anise in the pot, cover, and steep for 5 to 7 minutes. Strain and pour into a cup.

ORANGES

Oranges are high in vitamin C and pectin, which help lower cholesterol. They're powerfully anti-inflammatory, lower blood pressure, help with insulin resistance, and boost the immune system. Orange peel can relieve nausea, aid digestion, and clear mucus. Star anise, whether whole or seeds, helps with insomnia, asthma, infections, skin, eyes, and oral health, to name a few benefits.

FERMENTED TEA–KOMBUCHA

Kombucha is fermented tea water, and very tasty when infused with fruit or fruit juice. Kombucha has been around for many hundreds of years. Chinese medicine calls it the "immortal health elixir." Kombucha is made by fermenting a mixture of filtered water, organic sugar, and black, green, oolong, white, or rooibos tea. The fermentation culture is called a scoby. The final taste of this drink varies depending on the time allowed for fermentation and the infusion used. Kombucha has a mild vinegar taste and if left to ferment for too long, it will acquire a stronger taste. Infusing the tea after fermentation with fruit, juice, or herbs gives the brew additional artisanal flavor.

All cultured and fermented foods contain a small amount of naturally occurring alcohol. The alcohol in kombucha is normally 0.5 to 3 percent. The alcohol content can be higher when it is mixed with fruit or juice and allowed to sit for longer periods of time in a second fermentation.

Many health claims have been made for this elixir. They include treating arthritis, maintaining a healthy digestive tract, helping prevent and heal candida, fibromyalgia, depression, and bowel and stomach disorders. Kombucha is a natural detoxifier for the body and is rich in enzymes. It is a probiotic beverage that can indeed aid and improve digestion, remove harmful chemicals from the liver, and promote enzymes and good acids in the body.

It is really quite simple to make your own kombucha. Once you get started, you will understand that it only takes a few steps to create this amazingly healthy brew. Because the culture starter is alive, please read and follow the detailed instructions to ensure success.

WHAT IS A SCOBY?

Scoby (a.k.a. mother or mushroom) is an acronym for "symbiotic colony of bacteria and yeast." It is a starter culture necessary for making kombucha.

A scoby can form different pancake-like shapes. Some are smooth and rubbery, some may have holes, and others are lumpy and misshapen. They can be light brown, white, grayish, or beige. However they look, they are all good to use and all are "mothers" that will produce "babies" (this is where the term *mother* comes from). You need a scoby to start fermentation. When placed in the brewing tea, it may float to the top, sink, or hover in the liquid. It might produce strings of yeast that hang down into the liquid; strings may also form on the scoby itself. These attributes all describe a healthy scoby, as strange as it may seem.

Rarely will a scoby get moldy and have to be discarded. You will know when this happens, as the mold will be white or colorful and fuzzy. If the scoby dies, it will be black. Brown spots may appear on a scoby, but this is not mold. If a scoby gets moldy, toss out the whole batch of brew, including the scoby.

Kombucha cultures can be reused many times over. A new scoby will form in every batch of kombucha tea. When a batch of tea is finished and bottled, you can allow the babies to remain on the original scoby for the next brewing batch, or you can peel off the babies and pass them on to someone who may benefit from the healthy properties of kombucha. Scoby babies can also be composted along with older cultures. If babies are not peeled off the original scoby, the culture will thicken. This is not a problem unless the culture gets too difficult to handle. There are no benefits to a thicker or thinner scoby; you can always discard the babies. Keep in mind that a scoby will grow to the size of the container it is kept in. A scoby can be cut in half, preferably with a porcelain knife. If you don't have such a knife, be sure the knife you use is very clean. The scoby will heal over and form another scoby on top of the cut piece when placed in the tea brew.

If possible, get a starter from a friend who makes kombucha. A new scoby is formed with every batch and those of us who make our own kombucha are always looking for a home for baby scobys. If you are the first on your block to make kombucha, there are a few ways you can obtain a starter. You can order a scoby starter from a reputable online source, such as Cultures for Health, or you can start your own from scratch. Most health food stores carry commercial kombucha in a bottle. Be sure to save the balance of the starter tea, as doing so allows you to return the scoby to a safe place after the fermentation is complete.

Starting a scoby from a store-bought kombucha is very easy:

Purchase a bottle of kombucha.

Pour the kombucha into a large jar or glass bowl. Do not use a metal or plastic container.

Cover the container with cheesecloth or a clean, breathable kitchen towel.

Place a rubber band around the neck of the jar to secure the cloth.

Place the jar away from light for approximately 2 weeks.

The scoby will start to grow by forming a milky film in the liquid. The scoby will also thicken as days go by. The temperature in the room will determine how quickly the scoby grows; warmer temperatures produce a more rapidly growing scoby. When you see the scoby form into a disk (usually in about two weeks), it is time to brew tea and start the fermentation process.

For your fermentation to be successful, be mindful of your ingredients and other supplies:

It is not recommended to add brown sugar or honey to the mixture, as these ingredients may slow down or even stop the fermentation process.

All utensils that touch the kombucha should be clean and sterile, so as not to contaminate the brew. Do not use metal utensils.

Be sure to brew in a glass or porcelain jar. Do not use a plastic, stainless steel, or other metal jar.

Ingredients Needed for Making Kombucha

1 gallon filtered water

8 black, green, white, oolong, or rooibos tea bags, tags removed
(the strings can stay)

1 cup organic cane sugar

1 scoby

1 cup kombucha liquid from a prior batch, called a starter tea (will
come with the scoby when purchasing online); reserve any leftover
liquid for future uses

Fruit or herbs to flavor the kombucha for a second fermentation

Supplies Needed for Making Kombucha

One 1-gallon glass sun tea jar or ceramic vessel

A long-handled wooden spoon for stirring

Cheesecloth, nut milk bag, a clean paint strainer bag, or another clean
cloth that allows air to circulate. It should be large enough to fit
over the opening of the glass container.

A rubber band or string that is large (or small) enough to fit around the
neck of the bottle to secure the cloth

Several 8- to 12-ounce glass bottles with screw tops or airlock caps
(such as used for home-brewing beer)

A plastic strainer

BREWING TEA FOR KOMBUCHA

There are two methods for brewing the tea for kombucha. One method is to make a sun tea, using water that is not boiled; the other is to make a standard tea using boiled water. Regardless of which method is used, a scoby is added after the cooled tea is brewed.

THE SUN TEA METHOD: Fill a 1-gallon glass jar with filtered water. Place the tea bags in the jar. Add the organic cane sugar, stir well, and secure the lid. Set the jar in a sunny spot for a few hours, or until the tea darkens. Tea will be ready in a few hours if set in sunlight, longer if there is no sun.

THE BOILING METHOD: Lightly boil 2 quarts of filtered water in a pot, then add the organic cane sugar. Dissolve the sugar by stirring. Place the tea bags in the pot. Turn off the heat and let the mixture cool. Pour into a 1-gallon glass jar or ceramic vessel and add the remaining 2 quarts of filtered water. The tea must be cool before adding the scoby. When the water is completely cooled down, remove the tea bags.

FERMENTING THE TEA

Now that the tea is cooled down, slip the scoby into the jar along with the cup of starter tea the scoby was housed in. The process of adding the mature acidified liquid is important because it ensures that no mold forms. Once you place the scoby in the tea, the scoby might float to the top or drop to the bottom or lie on its side. Do not be concerned if it sinks to the bottom, as it will rise back up to the top in a couple of days.

Cover the jar with a piece of cheesecloth or any breathable cloth that allows air to circulate. The aim here is to keep pesky fruit flies or mold spores out of the brew. Put a rubber band or tie a string around the cloth at the neck of the jar to keep the cloth secure. Place the jar away from sunlight in a warm location, and put a sticker or tape on the jar with the date that the brew started. Dating the jar is important so you know how long the tea has been fermenting.

In 10 to 14 days, remove the cloth and taste the tea, using a wooden spoon. Metal is not advised, as it might contaminate the liquid. The kombucha should not taste too sweet or too vinegary. The warmer the temperature, the faster the kombucha ferments. During warmer times, check the kombucha in 5 to 6 days. When the sugar taste has dissipated, fermentation has taken place. Let your taste buds decide whether enough sugar has been converted. When you are happy with the fermented taste of the kombucha, it's ready to drink. You can decide at this time to bottle and refrigerate, or whether a second fermentation with flavoring is desired. A second fermentation increases the carbonation and lactic acid. It also adds a small amount to the alcohol content, totalling no more than 0.1 to 0.2 percent. For reference, beer contains about 4 percent alcohol and wine about 7 percent.

SECOND FERMENTATION

A second fermentation allows flavorings to be added to the kombucha, giving it a delicious taste while producing more carbonation. Any fruit, vegetable, or herb can be used to flavor kombucha. Flavoring kombucha adds more variety and enhances the taste. Sugars help kombucha fizz and carbonate, so using something sweet for flavoring is suggested.

Both frozen and fresh fruit work well. If using frozen fruit, place in a bowl and let it partially or thoroughly thaw. Use both the fruit and the liquid when marinating. If using fresh fruit, add directly to the bottle.

Cherries, raspberries, blackberries, strawberries, grapes, mango, pomegranate, ginger, and lemon all make delicious kombucha. Do not include the rind of citrus fruits, as citrus rinds give off a bitter taste.

Use your individual or clipped bottles for a variety of flavoring. Press 1 tablespoon of chosen fruits 1 tablespoon of juice into each bottle. Pour kombucha into bottle, filling it 1 inch from the top. Carbonation pressurizes the bottle and the bottle could explode if it is filled all the way to the top. At this point, close the lid and reserve 1 cup of liquid with your scoby.

After adding the flavoring, label the bottles with the flavor description. This allows you to remember what your favorite flavors are. If you plan to make another batch of kombucha immediately, add the date to the bottles, label so you know which batch of kombucha to consume first.

Set the bottles on the counter out of the way. It may take anywhere from 3 to 5 days for more carbonation to occur. Carbonation occurs more quickly in a warm room than a cool room, but either way is fine. Carefully release the tops once a day during this time. Taste to see whether the carbonation is to your liking. When desired level of carbonation is achieved, refrigerate the bottles. Although carbonation is slowed down once refrigerated, you may need to release the cap every couple of days. Open the bottles carefully—and do not shake—as the carbonation will not stop entirely.

HOW TO STORE A SCOBY WHEN NOT MAKING KOMBUCHA

Once you start making kombucha, you will more than likely make one batch after another. Eventually, however, you might have to stop. To keep your culture alive, it is best to leave it submerged in unflavored kombucha tea in a glass jar or container.

Cover the container with cheesecloth and secure it with a rubber band. Leave the container on the kitchen counter to ferment. The cheesecloth will allow the culture to breathe. This method is good if the time frame is less than 6 weeks. Longer breaks are a little more difficult to accomplish, but are not impossible. If you take a vacation from making kombucha for a period of time longer than 6 weeks and want to keep the scoby alive, leave the scoby in a full-size jar of brewed kombucha tea. When ready to use again, discard all but a starter cup of the brewed tea. The brew will have a strong vinegar taste. You might like to use the vinegar brew for making a salad dressing, or you may want to just toss it out. Another option for saving the scoby for more than several weeks is to keep a holding jar. This holding jar can sit on the kitchen counter. Every 4 to 6 weeks, discard some of the tea brew and put some fresh sugared tea in its place. Up to 80 percent replacement is fine. The fresh sugar will provide the scoby with all the nutrients it needs to survive. Freezing is not an option.

VIRGIN KOMBUCHA MOJITO

Inspired by The Seed, Port Andratx, Mallorca, Spain

INGREDIENTS

3 mint sprigs, plus a pinch of mint for garnish

8 ounces kombucha

2 ounces fresh lime juice

1 or 2 dashes of sparkling soda

Simple maple syrup (page 168; optional)

½ cup or more ice cubes

2 lime slices

METHOD

Place the mint in a tall glass or pitcher and muddle it with the back of a wooden spoon to break down the oils. Add the kombucha, lime juice, soda, and syrup and stir well. Taste and adjust, if necessary. Add ice, lime slices, and a pinch of mint to garnish. If you assemble the mojito in a 16-ounce mason jar, proceed as directed, but place the ice directly in a serving glass and pour the drink over the ice, then add the lime slices and mint garnish.

PARTY TIME

Many times at parties there are tubs filled with ice and cans of soda and plastic bottles of water for guests to help themselves to a drink. What if your guests find tubs filled with 8-ounce mason or Ball jars that contain cold brew fruit infusions! These jars look inviting, the drinks are delicious, and they are loaded with health benefits. Even alcohol drinkers need to stay hydrated at a party. You can find lids to fit these jars that have a hole on the top. Built-in or inserted straws add to the ease of drinking the cold brew infusions.

The night before your party, simply select the flavor of tea bags you want and place one in each 8-ounce jar. If you have plenty of 8-ounce jars on hand, you can just order the lids from Amazon or other online sellers. These jars are perfect for a party. Add a variety of seasonal fruit, fill each jar with filtered water, and screw on its lid. Refrigerate for 6 hours or overnight. When the time arrives for the party, fill a large ice container with crushed or chunked ice, remove the tea bags, and half-bury jars in the ice. Place an ice tong in the ice container as well, so guests can add ice to their cold brew, if desired. Another simple idea is to prepare quart- or half-gallon jars of tea, then pour into 8-ounce party jars and infuse with a variety of assorted fruits and herbs, such as kiwi, strawberries, and so forth. When making larger amounts, a good-quality loose tea can be used; strain out the loose tea before serving.

Have handy a container of simple syrup, should anyone need sweetener. Standard simple syrup is made with cane sugar and water and heated until the sugar is dissolved, but using maple syrup and water makes a healthier version of simple syrup.

Simple Maple Syrup

Lightly heat two parts water to one part pure maple syrup and stir until the syrup dissolves into the water. Taste for sweetness and adjust as necessary. Remove from the heat, allow to cool, and place in an easy-pour or squeeze bottle container.

Cold Brew Refrigerator Tea Combinations

After making a few cold brew batches, you will find there are countless ways to express yourself and be creative. Here are some recipe ideas to get you started on the road to health and hydration.

Fill your jar with the chosen tea bag or loose tea and cold brew overnight. In the morning, remove the bags or loose tea and add:

INGREDIENTS

A splash of fruit juice

A handful of berries + a sprig of fresh mint

Slices of orange + several blackberries + a few basil leaves

Orange slices or dried orange peels + several blueberries + a sprig of fresh thyme

Peach slices + a sprig of mint

Citrus zest or citrus slices

Diced dried fruit

Chopped or sliced stone fruit

Organic edible flowers

Fresh herbs, such as sage, rosemary, basil, or parsley

Dried Orange, Lemon, Lime, or Grapefruit Peels

There are various ways to prepare citrus for drying. Always use organic citrus and wash and dry the fruit. One method is to use a sharp vegetable peeler to peel the rind off the fruit in thin strips, leaving the white pith behind. Another way is to uniformly slice the whole fruit, keeping the flesh of the fruit intact and just removing the seeds.

Dried peels are best stored in an airtight glass container for up to 3 months in the refrigerator. If filling tea bags, place the dried peels in a food processor and pulse to chop to the desired size.

DEHYDRATOR METHOD: Wash, dry, and peel or slice the fruit. Place the peels or slices on the mesh screen, not touching one another and set the dehydrator temperature to 100°F. Dry for about 20 hours or longer, until the strips are curled and feel dry to the touch. Remove from the dehydrator and allow to cool before storing in an airtight glass container in the refrigerator.

OVEN METHOD: Preheat the oven to its lowest temperature; 200°F is fine. Wash, dry, and peel or slice the fruit. Place the peels or slices on a parchment-lined baking sheet in a single layer, not touching one another. Bake for 30 or more minutes, until they start to curl and harden. The drying time varies, so check after 30 minutes to see whether your peels are ready. Remove from the oven and allow to cool before storing in an airtight glass container in the refrigerator.

Tea- and Fruit-Infused Ice Cubes

You will love making these simple recipes to enhance your cold brew infusions. Infused ice cubes bring any cold drink to life. They can give a lovely frosty look and sweet taste to your cold brews, as well as add more health to your drink. Their look, taste, and benefits give your drinks a pop of perfection. Fancy ice cubes take minutes to make and their cost is almost free. They are always a big hit at parties for adults and children alike. Purchase easy-to-release silicone ice cube trays online or from a kitchen supply store; they come in a variety of shapes and sizes.

Use filtered water or leftover cold brew infusions. For lightly colored cubes, use light-colored teas, such as mint, green, or white tea, so you can still see the herb or fruit infusion. To make more strongly flavored ice cubes, use more tea bags when brewing. In this way, your drink won't be watered down.

Clear ice cubes show off the fruit or herb infusion best, but so many times infused ice cubes appear frosted or opaque. Here is the secret of how to get clear ice cubes: It's all in the water and the cooling method. You must use filtered water and lightly boil it. Boiling removes most of the dissolved air. Boil the water, let it cool, and lightly boil again. Not a hard boil, just a tiny-bubble boil is best. After the second boil, let the water cool down, add your fresh or frozen fruit or herbs to the ice cube tray, and pour the cooled water on top to fill. Freeze immediately for 5 to 6 hours or overnight.

To add a pop of color, boost your immunity, and add other health benefits to your cold brew infusions, use unsweetened bottled juice or fresh-squeezed fruit juice to make ice cubes. These beautiful colored ice cubes will enhance any cold brew or plain filtered water. Picture pomegranate, grape, blueberry, pineapple, or strawberry juice cubes, to name just a few. For iced lattes, try freezing almond milk sweetened with a little pure maple syrup. This will give your iced latte a chill without diluting the flavor.

HOW TO MAKE INFUSED ICE CUBES: Here are several methods for making infused ice cubes. If you use the first or second method, try half-filling, so more of the fruit, herb, or flower is exposed. A squeeze bottle is handy to fill the ice trays so the liquid doesn't run over the sides. A steady hand works as well.

- Fill the ice cube tray compartments with your selected fruit, herb, or flower, then fill the tray with cooled-down, twice-boiled water.
- Fill the ice cube tray compartments with your selected fruit, herb, or flower, then fill the tray with cold brew tea.
- Fill the ice cube tray compartments with juice and place one of your selected fruit, herb, or flower on top, immersed just a bit in the water. Edible flowers, cherries with stems attached and sticking above the frozen cube, or triangular slices of fruit all make beautiful ice cubes. The choices are endless.
- Freeze for 5 to 6 hours or overnight. Once the cubes are frozen, transfer them to a freezer bag, label with the flavor of the cubes, and store in the freezer. Work quickly when transferring the cubes to the bag, so they don't melt and stick together when refrozen.
- Add ice cubes to cold brew infusions or filtered water for a delightful experience.

TIP: Place frozen fruit juice ice cubes into a blender and blitz to make shaved ice for a frosted drink. Frozen shaved ice makes a yummy, healthy treat for children as well.

Ice Cube Infusions with Healthy Properties, Colors, and Flavors

Blueberries	Mint leaf
Blackberries	Italian parsley leaf
Mango cube	Small basil leaf
Peach slice	Sage leaf
Pineapple wedge	Thyme stem
Pomegranate seeds	Rosemary stem
Sliced strawberries	Edible flowers
Raspberries	Green tea
Segment of a lime slice	Pineapple juice
Segment of a lemon slice	Cranberry juice
Segment of an orange slice	Lemonade
Twist of lemon zest	Orange juice

TEAS, HERBAL INFUSIONS, AND THEIR HEALTH BENEFITS

Drinking tea is very hydrating and that alone can help with many health issues, as hydration is a cornerstone of good health. For me, teas are a miracle elixir, as all teas have additional health benefits.

Whether hot or cold, tea may help treat many ailments. Drinking tea or herbal infusions boost our T cells' ability to fight against viral and bacterial infections, such as colds or flu. One of the key components of tea that promotes better health is the polyphenols found in green, black, oolong, and white tea. Polyphenols are plant-derived compounds that boost the immune system and may help the body protect against disease. In addition, almost all teas are loaded with powerful antioxidants that may rid the body of inflammation. And herbal teas, which come in a variety of flavors, are delicious and nourishing.

Drinking at least 32 ounces of cold brew or hot tea daily could have a positive impact on your health. Teas can help make significant changes to your overall well-being, mood, skin, energy, and so on. There are a vast variety of tea and herbal infusions, each containing different properties, which work best for specific issues. For example, some teas are known to improve brain function, aid in fat loss, reduce insomnia, or clear your skin.

Any of the teas in each category in this section can be combined for taste or potency; for example, ginger and turmeric, green and herbal infusion, or oolong and blackberries. Also, note that health food stores and online tea companies sell blends of teas for particular issues, such as Cold Cure, Breath Easy, Throat Coat, Everyday Detox, and many others.

If you are drinking tea to help with your health, I suggest you resist adding sugar. Drinking four to six cups or glasses of sweetened tea daily could add up to too much sugar.

Please note that these teas may support organ function or help relieve symptoms, but *may not on their own prevent or cure a listed ailment.* Do not stop any current medication or rely solely on tea for your health without consulting your doctor. Also, always consult your doctor if you are pregnant or taking medications, before making tea drinking a regular part of your diet.

By Ailment

ALLERGIES–stinging nettle, rooibos, chamomile, green, licorice root, ginger, lemon balm, peppermint, and turmeric

ALZHEIMER'S–green, black, *Ginkgo biloba*, rosemary, sage, kava, gotu kola, oolong, white, and yerba maté

ANEMIA–dandelion, hibiscus, chamomile, cinnamon, clove, guarana, nettle, peppermint, and raspberry

ANTIAGING AND LONGEVITY–green, black, white, oolong, rooibos, peach, orange, raspberry, chamomile, pomegranate, lady's mantle, *Ginkgo biloba*, and rosemary

ANTIBACTERIAL/ANTIMICROBIAL–pu-erh, hops, kava, skullcap, rosebud, echinacea, and dandelion

ANTI-INFLAMMATORY–hops, kava, skullcap, green, black, white, oolong, rooibos, hibiscus, raspberry, jasmine, alfalfa, chamomile, rose hip, lady's mantle, ginger, rosebud, stinging nettle, rosemary, and sage

ANXIETY–hibiscus, passionflower, hops, kava, skullcap, chamomile, borage, rosemary, jasmine, lemon balm, lavender, peppermint, valerian, rosebud, and green

ARTHRITIS–aloe vera, boswellia, eucalyptus, green, turmeric, chamomile, rosemary, and ginger

ASTHMA–rooibos, passionflower, sage, ginger, echinacea, and turmeric

BACTERIAL INFECTION–green, black, white, oolong, ginger, echinacea, garlic, goldenseal, sage, peppermint, and chamomile

BAD BREATH–green, black, spearmint, Moroccan mint, peppermint, parsley, and rosemary

BLADDER–green, black, goldenrod, cranberry, parsley, peppermint, and dandelion

BRAIN FUNCTION–green, black, oolong, white, yerba maté, *Ginkgo biloba*, sage, gotu kola, ginger, turmeric, and rosemary

BRONCHITIS–ginger, echinacea, thyme, elderberry, eucalyptus, goldenseal, lemon peel, nettle, peppermint, rooibos, and rose hip

BLOATING–alfalfa, ginger, peppermint, dandelion, fennel, lavender, chamomile, and green

BONE HEALTH–oolong, rooibos, green, black, white, Darjeeling, and pu-erh

CALMING–chamomile, jasmine, green, lemon balm, lavender, peppermint, kava, valerian, rosebud, passion flower, hibiscus, hops, and skullcap

CANCER–Some claims have been made that certain teas may help in the prevention of cancer, however, there are not enough studies at this time to back up these claims. Teas that continue to be tested include green, black, oolong, and white.

CARDIOVASCULAR DISEASE–green, black, white, oolong, chamomile, rose hip, and *Ginkgo biloba*

CELLULAR HEALTH–green, black, white, oolong, *Ginkgo biloba*, chamomile, valerian, peppermint, ginger, hawthorn berry, and milk thistle

CHOLESTEROL–white, green, black, oolong, hibiscus, jasmine, pu-erh, chamomile, pomegranate, and *Ginkgo biloba*

CIRCULATION–green, black, spearmint, orange, white, oolong, *Ginkgo biloba*, gotu kola, ginger, and parsley

COLDS–black, green, cinnamon, echinacea, gotu kola, nettle, borage, lemongrass, ginger, sage, and lemon verbena

COLITIS–green, ginger, mint, turmeric, calendula, fennel, and slippery elm

CONCENTRATION–green, black, white, oolong, *Ginkgo biloba*, alfalfa, gotu kola, and rosemary

CONGESTION–Moroccan mint, lemon, ginger, peppermint, eucalyptus, chamomile, thyme, black, anise, cinnamon, echinacea, gotu kola, nettle, and borage

CYSTITIS–cranberry, green, turmeric, ginger, dandelion, and turmeric

DENTAL HEALTH, TEETH AND GUMS–green, black, orange, white, oolong, echinacea, rooibos, stinging nettle, Darjeeling, and peach

DETOXIFIER–pu-erh, rose hip, *Ginkgo biloba*, borage, burdock, milk thistle, dandelion, garlic, ginger, and cilantro

DIABETES, TYPE 2–green, Moroccan mint, white, black, jasmine, oolong, chamomile, stinging nettle, dandelion, and sage

DIARRHEA–raspberry, blackberry, chamomile, stinging nettle, peppermint, and fennel

DIGESTION–chai, Moroccan mint, spearmint, rooibos, green, black, Darjeeling, hibiscus, passionflower, jasmine, pu-erh, ginger, dandelion, chamomile, lavender, peppermint, rosemary, and parsley

DIURETIC–green, black, alfalfa, dandelion, hibiscus, anise, chamomile, ginger, rosebud, parsley, and hibiscus

ECZEMA–green, chamomile, yerba maté, and rooibos

EDEMA–parsley, dandelion, *Ginkgo biloba*, and cranberry

ENERGIZING–green, black, oolong, white, rooibos, yerba maté, ginger, *Ginkgo biloba*, rose hip, and ginseng

EYE HEALTH–green, black, oolong, white, eyebright, calendula, peach, *Ginkgo biloba*, and fennel. To relax your eyes from stress, cooled tea bags can be placed directly on closed eyelids for 15 minutes.

FATIGUE–green, black, oolong, white, rooibos, yerba maté, ginger, *Ginkgo biloba*, rose hip, and ginseng

FEVER–borage, stinging nettle, chamomile, peppermint, spearmint, ginger, and yarrow

FIBROMYALGIA–green, black, oolong, white, passionflower, turmeric, and ginger

FLU–cinnamon, ginger, stinging nettle, lemon balm, turmeric, lemon verbena, green, black, peppermint, yerba maté, rose hip, and hibiscus

GALLBLADDER/GALLSTONES–green, turmeric, milk thistle, chamomile, parsley, ginger, peppermint, and dandelion

GAS AND GASTROINTESTINAL–green, black, rooibos, Moroccan mint, peppermint, spearmint, ginger, chamomile, fennel, Darjeeling, raspberry, anise, cinnamon, lemon balm, dandelion, stinging nettle, and licorice

GOUT–green, chamomile, stinging nettle, milk thistle, and hibiscus

HAIR HEALTH–green, black, oolong, lady's mantle, stinging nettle, rosemary, lemongrass, lavender, ginger, and kombucha

HEADACHES–ginger, rooibos, passionflower, chamomile, *Ginkgo biloba*, and peppermint

HEART–green, oolong, white, black, Moroccan mint, chamomile, Darjeeling, raspberry, orange, passionflower, jasmine, and alfalfa

HORMONE BALANCING–green, raspberry, oolong, white, black, stinging nettle, *Ginkgo biloba*, chamomile, licorice, orange peel, cranberry, red clover, yarrow, and lady's mantle

HYPERACTIVITY/ADHD–lemon balm, skullcap, ginseng, chamomile, valerian, licorice, lavender, *Ginkgo biloba*, gotu kola, spearmint, and lemongrass

HYPERTENSION–Moroccan mint, white, rooibos, green, black, hibiscus, passionflower, oolong, chamomile, pomegranate, pomegranate, and rosemary

IMMUNE SYSTEM–chai, spearmint, rooibos, black, hibiscus, raspberry, jasmine, green, white, oolong, rose hip, peppermint, and echinacea

INSOMNIA–rooibos, passionflower, valerian, chamomile, lemon balm, hops, kava, skullcap, passionflower, and lavender

IRRITABLE BOWEL SYNDROME–anise, fennel, dandelion, ginger, licorice, stinging nettle, lavender, peppermint, chamomile, and turmeric

JOINT PAIN–eucalyptus, cat's claw, green, turmeric, chamomile, rosemary, and ginger

KIDNEY AND KIDNEY STONES–goldenrod, black, green, cranberry, parsley, peppermint, dandelion, and stinging nettle

LIVER–hibiscus, dandelion, peppermint, turmeric, fennel, rosemary, milk thistle, burdock, ginger, and green

LUNGS–stinging nettle, peppermint, oregano, peppermint, eucalyptus, hawthorn, and thyme

MEMORY–gotu kola, green, *Ginkgo biloba*, sage, black, oolong, white, yerba maté, ginger, turmeric, and rosemary

MENSTRUAL CRAMPS–passionflower, lavender, mint, lady's mantle, *Ginkgo biloba*, and stinging nettle

MENTAL CLARITY AND PERFORMANCE–Moroccan mint, green, black, oolong, white, cinnamon, gotu kola, *Ginkgo biloba*, sage, yerba maté, ginger, turmeric, and rosemary

NAUSEA–peppermint, raspberry, anise, ginger, and spearmint

OSTEOPENIA/OSTEOPOROSIS–green, white, oolong, black, rooibos, Darjeeling, and pu-erh

PANCREATITIS–dandelion, turmeric, milk thistle, and licorice

PARKINSON'S–matcha, black, white, and green

PSORIASIS–green, black, oolong, lemon, ginger, slippery elm, milk thistle, and rooibos

RHEUMATISM–green, borage, goldenrod, burdock, turmeric, ginger, rose hip, black, willow bark, and nettle

ROSACEA–green, lavender, chamomile, yerba maté, rooibos, sage, calendula, chamomile, rose hip, and lady's mantle

SINUS–ginger, echinacea, thyme, elderberry, eucalyptus, goldenseal, lemon peel, nettle, peppermint, rooibos, and rose hip

SKIN DISORDERS–Moroccan mint, green, black, peach, oolong, borage, calendula, chamomile, rose hip, lady's mantle, stinging nettle, rosemary, and sage

SORE THROAT–anise, echinacea, eucalyptus, passionflower, lady's mantle, goldenseal, peppermint, and sage

STRESS REDUCER–chamomile, spearmint, Moroccan mint, rooibos, jasmine, hops, kava, skullcap, lavender, lemon balm, passion flower, sage, and borage

THYROID–chamomile, green, chicory, sage, tulsi, elderberry, astragalus, and chicory root

TOXEMIA–raspberry leaf, nettle, ginger, dandelion, peppermint, lemon balm, rooibos, and lady's mantle

URINARY TRACT INFECTION–green, goldenrod, cat's claw, milk thistle, and lady's mantle

WEIGHT LOSS–green, black, Darjeeling, oolong, hibiscus, orange, raspberry, jasmine, white, pu-erh, borage, rose hip, ginger, rooibos, pomegranate, lady's mantle, peppermint, stinging nettle, and sage. A healthy diet and exercise along with tea, can provide some results.

By Tea

ALFALFA TEA–Alfalfa tea is used for high cholesterol, upset stomach, asthma, diabetes, and arthritis. It contains vitamins A, C, and E, and phosphorous, calcium, potassium, and iron.

BLACK TEA–Known to lower the risk of diabetes and heart disease, regulates blood sugar, contains anti-inflammatory properties, lowers LDL, may improve gut health, and reduces blood pressure and risk of stroke.

BORAGE TEA–Good for arthritis, congestion, cough, menstrual cramps, depression, hormone balancing, and colds.

BURDOCK TEA–Contains powerful antioxidants, including quercetin, luteolin, and phenolic acids. Burdock tea is good for removing toxins from the body, helps with skin issues, protects the cells against free radicals, and reduces inflammation.

CHAI–Chai is a mixture of black tea, herbs, and spices and contains all the benefits of black tea along with such additions as ginger, cinnamon, cardamom, fennel, and black pepper. This tea contains anti-inflammatory properties and is high in antioxidants. Chai will give your immune system a boost, help relieve indigestion, and could aid in weight loss.

CHAMOMILE TEA–Known for its calming properties; relieves stress and promotes sleep. Chamomile helps lessen premenstrual symptoms, is good for digestion, and helps lower high blood lipids, blood sugar, and insulin levels. It works as an antibacterial and anti-inflammatory aide, and has liver-protecting effects. This tea helps fight diarrhea and stomach ulcers as well as soothes coughs and bronchitis symptoms.

DANDELION TEA–Helps lessen hot flashes, combats kidney stones, and is a gentle way to cleanse and regenerate the liver and the blood. Dandelion tea is popular because it acts as a diuretic to stimulate digestion.

ECHINACEA TEA–Echinacea helps build the immune system. It may help prevent or ease the common cold. It sooths coughs, sore throat, and congestion. Echinacea keeps you teeth strong and is used as a dental pain reliever.

ELDERBERRY TEA–This tea is immunity-boosting; aids in colds, fever, and flu; and helps remove toxins from the body.

EYEBRIGHT TEA–Good for eyes, colds, allergies, earaches, headache, sinusitis, and sore throat.

***GINKGO BILOBA* TEA**–High in antioxidants, fights inflammation; improves heart health and circulation; reduces anxiety, depression, and stress; improves brain function; supports eye health; improves asthma; and eases menstrual cramps.

GINGER TEA–Used for hot flashes, menopausal issues, nausea, motion sickness, allergies, and muscle aches and cramps. Ginger relieves indigestion constipation and is a detoxifier. It also helps fight inflammation and stimulates the immune system.

GOLDENROD TEA–Reduces inflammation, reduces joint pain and swelling, works as a diuretic, stops muscle spasms, and is used for gout, arthritis, and eczema and other skin conditions. It relieves asthma and hay fever, and supports urinary tract health.

GOTU KOLA TEA–Used to treat viral or bacterial urinary tract infections. It is also used to treat influenza, dysentery, colds, flu, shingles, anxiety, and depression, and improves memory, circulation, stomach pain, and diarrhea.

GREEN TEA–High in antioxidants, promotes healthy cell growth, lowers LDL, relaxes the body, stimulates the brain, inhibits carcinogenic effect of processed foods, and contains powerful antioxidants called polyphenols, which fight free radicals and stop the damage they cause.

HIBISCUS TEA–Hibiscus tea is naturally high in vitamin and antioxidants. It can be used as a diuretic, and also gives a refreshed feeling. Hibiscus is known to lower high blood pressure and cholesterol, and to strengthen the immune system and help fight off flu.

JASMINE TEA–Jasmine tea is high in antioxidants and anti-inflammatory properties, which may promote heart health. It is good for skin problems, and may boost your immune system, increase your energy, help with weight loss, and relieve stress, aches, and pains.

LAVENDER TEA–Used for anxiety, stress, depression, and restlessness. It relieves coughs, colds, fever, insomnia, joint stiffness, sore muscles, and rheumatic pain. Spray lavender tea on your skin to repel bugs.

MOROCCAN MINT TEA–Moroccan mint tea is made with green tea, so it has all the benefits of green tea as well as mint. Is a powerful antioxidant and can boost mental performance, focus, and endurance and protects against cardiovascular disease. This tea can loosens congestion and alleviate nasal allergies, and acts as a mild sedative. It is good for skin disorders, digestion, headaches, and improves breath. It cools the body in summer, inhibits growth of bacteria, and is a good blood cleanser.

OOLONG TEA–Oolong tea is close in health properties to green and black, but may not be as well known. With its high antioxidants and loads on nutrients, vitamins, and amino acids, which include manganese, potassium, magnesium, niacin, and caffeine, oolong may boost metabolism and reduce stress. Oolong tea may reduce blood sugar and insulin levels, and promote heart health. This tea may help decrease the risk of high blood pressure in some people. Since oolong tea boosts the metabolism, it may decrease the amount of fat absorbed from your diet and help burn more calories per day. Oolong has been said to improve brain function and promote teeth and bone strength. Oolong may help relieve eczema and other skin irritations.

PASSION FRUIT TEA–Traditionally used to relieve anxiety and irritability, and improves sleep by promoting calmness. It improves cardiovascular health, boosts immunity, improves digestion, reduces inflammation, and helps with skin conditions.

PEPPERMINT TEA–Anti-inflammatory, peppermint settles an upset stomach, such as bloating, gas, and cramps; is good for nausea, and vomiting. This tea is a decongestant and helps suppress appetite. Relieves stress and muscle spasms. Peppermint will warm up the body and make you sweat, which will remove's toxins from the body. It is helpful for IBS or gallstones. Not recommended for heartburn or indigestion.

PU-ERH TEA–Because of its caffeine content, pu-erh may increase your energy, but it may also help promote heart health and bone strength, and may be used as a detoxifier. It is high in antioxidants and vitamin C, so pu-erh is good to drink during colds and flu season. This tea is antibacterial and anti-inflammatory. Because it's related to green, black, oolong, and white teas, it may lower cholesterol and blood sugar. Pu-erh aids digestion and improve sleep.

RASPBERRY LEAF TEA–Although this tea is known as a woman's tea as it's used to strengthen the uterine wall, it's also a good tea for men. It helps with hormone balancing and contains nutrients and antioxidants. Raspberry leaf tea is rich in vitamins, including B complex and C, and potassium, magnesium, zinc, and iron. It improves digestion and soothes the lungs and an irritated throat. You can use this tea as a gargle as well. Raspberry leaf tea contains anti-inflammatory properties that help gums, mouth, and skin issues.

ROOIBOS TEA–Rooibos has high levels of antioxidants and important minerals, including calcium, iron, magnesium, and zinc. This tea may improve blood pressure and circulation. It helps relieve acne and skin conditions. Rooibos promotes relaxation and restful sleep. It's effective for allergies and kidney stones and may benefit bone health. Claims say this tea lowers markers of inflammation and cell toxicity. Rooibos may be good for the heart by lowering LDL cholesterol while increasing HDL. It also promotes bone health and works for appetite control and digestion, and to boost your immune system. Because of its high antioxidant content, this tea is used to slow down the aging process as it seeks out free radicals that damage the skin, hair, and bones that make us vulnerable to diseases. Rooibos tea may also help reduce the impact of oxidative by products in neural pathways, which may help prevent cognitive degeneration.

ROSE HIP TEA–Rose hip tea is rich in vitamin C and flavonoids, which makes this tea an immune supporter and skin enhancer. Rose hip aids the adrenal glands and helps combat colds and flu. The antioxidant properties help with heart disease, arthritis, and damage done by free radicals, which play a role in premature aging.

ROSEMARY TEA–This tea is rich in antioxidants and contains anti-inflammatory compounds. Rosemary tea's possible health benefits include improved memory and concentration, and it may slow down brain aging. This tea supports the immune system and blood circulation. This tea helps fight free radicals and improves digestion. Rosemary tea relieves stress and has a calming effect. Rosemary tea may also helpful in affecting the outer retina, which is affected by macular degeneration.

SAGE TEA–Sage has been used for sore throat, colds, and cough relief. It helps reduce anxiety and problems with digesting and ease menopausal symptoms. This tea is known for helping induce mental clarity and concentration. Sage tea contains powerful antioxidants and anti-inflammatory properties and is loaded with other vitamins and nutrients. Sage tea helps detoxify the body and combat the effects of free radicals. It also helps reduce cholesterol, regulates blood glucose, and may help improve cognitive function. It is best to combine sage with other teas that have a more palatable taste. It's worth the effort to consume sage tea for all its healing properties.

SKULLCAP TEA–High in antioxidants, skullcap tea benefits anxiety, depression, and headaches and aids in tension relief. This tea may help with insomnia and sleep disorders. Skullcap tea has been used to soothe the symptoms of alcohol and drug withdrawal, including muscle aches or twitches, digestive issues, and stress. Because of large amounts of flavonoids in skullcap tea, it is used for menstrual cramps and other PMS symptoms. This tea may help relieve asthma, hay fever, and other nasal allergies. Skullcap tea can reduce inflammation, which will help in injury recovery and body wound healing.

SPEARMINT TEA–Spearmint tea is high in antioxidants, which help protect against and repair damage to our cells and body caused by free radicals. This tea is good for digestion issues and upset stomach. Spearmint tea may help with hormonal imbalances and fights bacterial infections. Drinking two or three cups a day may lower blood sugar and stress. Spearmint tea has shown beneficial effects on arthritis pain and may help lower blood pressure.

STINGING NETTLE TEA–Contains many nutrients including vitamins A, C, K, and several B vitamins. Stinging nettle also contains minerals, amino acids, and flavonoids. This tea combats seasonal allergies, eases arthritis, is an energy booster, and relieves itchy, watery eyes, sneezing, and runny nose. Stinging nettle reduces inflammation, which may help with arthritis pain. Stinging nettle may be beneficial in treating prostate gland enlargement. This tea may help your blood vessels to relax, which may reduce blood pressure.

THYME TEA–Contains antioxidants, vitamin and minerals, making this an all-over feel-good tea. Potential benefits include helping fight inflammation, and bacteria, and promoting healthy blood pressure. Use this tea for coughs, congestion, and to build your immune system. This tea is good for digestion and may help weight loss.

TULSI TEA, A.K.A. HOLY BASIL–Good to sip for respiratory disorders. Tulsi relieves stress and regulates blood sugar levels. Its anti-inflammatory properties my help with arthritis pain. Sipping this tea can help get rid of headaches, aid in cardiovascular problems, help digestion, reduce fevers, dissolve kidney stones, and benefit dental and oral health.

VALERIAN ROOT TEA–The most well-known benefit of valerian root tea is its sleep-enhancing effect. This tea may also help relieve anxiety and stress. It's said that valerian root can help with menstrual cramps and hot flashes. Because of its sedative effect, it is not recommend to drink with alcohol or when driving, and do not drink valerian tea if you are taking other sleep medication.

WHITE TEA–Like green, black. and oolong tea, white tea is rich in antioxidants. Drinking this tea may reduce the risk of heart disease, help protect your mouth from bacteria, and lower the risk of insulin resistance. This tea may also be good for your bones, and may combat skin aging. Because of its high antioxidant properties and compounds, including the polyphenol EGCG, both white and green tea may help arteries, cognition, and cell damage, which in turn may have an impact that minimizes the effects of Alzheimer's.

YERBA MATÉ TEA–May help respiratory issues, lower lipids, and lower blood pressure and cholesterol. This tea works to produce corticosteroids, which act as an anti-inflammatory, and it can give you a balanced energy boost and can clear your mind. Yerba maté is known to be good for bone health, indigestion, and circulation, and contains anti-inflammatory benefits.

ACKNOWLEDGMENTS

Having a great agent and publisher is half the job of putting out a good book. I have both. Thanks to Kari Stuart of ICM Partners and her team for always being there for me. Much gratitude to my publisher, The Countryman Press at W. W. Norton & Company. I'm thankful to work with Ann Treistman, editorial director, who has taught me so much. We have worked together on six of my books and she is always invaluable to the process. Thank you to the amazing Aurora Bell, associate editor at Countryman, who walked me through my last few books.

When I'm writing, I'm totally absorbed in my work. My closest ally, Mike Mendell, who I spend my days and nights with, is patient beyond words. He is also the photographer for my books. I can't thank him enough for his love and kindness. My other ally is my daughter Lisa who is always there to read my work and give her honest opinion and feedback. All my children, Jonas, Mia, and Dan, and my grandchildren, Mackenzie, Hannah, Karly, Rocky, Luke, Audrey, and Gunner, and my daughter-in-law, Gigi, are my joy and inspiration for my writing. A shout-out to my dear friends, Julie, Sue, Cat, Victoria (who contributed a few photos to this book), Miriam, and Diana, who keep me laughing and are always supportive cheerleaders. I want to thank all my supporters on social media who continue to purchase my books, which makes it possible for me to keep writing. Half of this book was written in Mallorca, Spain, and half in San Diego, California. Last but not least, thanks to all my girlfriends in Spain who tea tested for me and to cat-faith.com retreats.

CREDITS

INDEX